KINGSFORD COMPLETE GRILLING COOKBOOK

KINGSFORD COMPLETE GRILLING COOKBOOK

RICK RODGERS

PHOTOGRAPHY BY BEN FINK

John Wiley & Sons, Inc.

For general information on our other products and services or for technical support, please contact our Customer Care Department within the United States at (800) 762-2974, outside the United States at (317) 572-3993 or fax (317) 572-4002.

Wiley also publishes its books in a variety of electronic formats. Some content that appears in print may not be available in electronic books. For more information about Wiley products, visit our web site at www.wiley.com.

Food styling by Megan Fawn Schlow. Prop styling by Barb Fritz.

Library of Congress Cataloging-in-Publication Data:

Rodgers, Rick, 1953-
  Kingsford complete grilling cookbook / Rick Rodgers.
     p. cm.
  Includes index.
  ISBN: 978-0-470-07914-0 (pbk.)
  1. Barbecue cookery. I. Title.
  TX840.B3R6157 2007
  641.7'6—dc22
                                        2006023010

Printed in the United States of America

10 9 8 7 6 5 4 3 2

CONTENTS

INTRODUCTION

Cooking always engages your senses, but charcoal grilling really gets them involved. You hear the sizzle of the meat on the grill, smell the smoke wafting up, see the grill marks seared onto the food and the appetizing brown crust developing, and touch the food to check for doneness. Above all, it is the taste that makes charcoal-grilled food unique—that mouthwatering smokiness that you just can't get from any other cooking method or source of heat.

Grilling, or at least cooking over fire, has been around for almost as long as humans have been eating. Today's cooks don't prepare food over a fire because it's the only way—they have many other good reasons. First, grilling is fun, and, as mentioned before, it makes food taste delicious. Maybe it is the social aspect of outdoor cooking that makes grilling so appealing, for grilling is well known for bringing people together for special occasions—what is the Fourth of July without a barbecue? (It should be said here and now that while the term *barbecue* has evolved to mean an outdoor cooking event and any kind of grilled food, to grilling experts, it specifically refers to the slow-smoked method so popular in the American South.)

Grilling has changed a lot over the years. There have been many studies tracking cooking trends, and they all show that cooking with charcoal has increased, even as other methods are introduced. That's no surprise, as nothing, I repeat *nothing*, can duplicate the flavor of food cooked over a charcoal fire.

Other statistics show that eight out of ten American households own a grill and that there is increased grill usage, including year-round grilling. The average amount of money spent on a grill has gone up as people want models with more bells and whistles. For many cooks, grilling is a passion, not just a way to put a hot dog in a bun.

Kingsford has been at the forefront of outdoor cooking since the 1920s. Even way back then, when Henry Ford opened the first Kingsford charcoal plant, the briquets were sold in bags with $2 grills. After World War II, when the GI Bill made purchasing homes with backyards easier and kettle charcoal grills hit the stores, outdoor grilling really took off. Now over one billion pounds of Kingsford® charcoal is used every year to fire up over three hundred million meals a year. And Kingsford has many other products that make charcoal grilling not only fun but easy—charcoal lighter fluid, wood chips, briquets with wood, and more.

Kingsford Complete Grilling Cookbook is for anytime you want to serve up a platter of smoke-kissed grilled food, from a weeknight supper to a holiday turkey. There's hardly a limit to what you can cook on the grill. Meat lovers are also grill lovers, and hamburgers, steaks, and hot dogs, along with chicken, are the most popular grilled foods, and they are well represented here. However, more and more people are cooking vegetables on the grill, too, both as side dishes and as main courses. You may be surprised to find grilled desserts in this book, including brownies and cobblers, but give these luscious treats a try. And we haven't neglected the side dishes that make an outdoor meal into a party, such as potato salad, fresh-squeezed lemonade, and others.

In addition to great recipes, *Kingsford Complete Grilling Cookbook* teaches you how to grill. There are plenty of variables with grilling, which is one of the things that make it so enjoyable and an engagement of the senses, so understanding the details ensures success. We'll show you the best way to build a charcoal fire, how to control the heat, how to choose the best grilling method for the food at hand, how to grill safely, and more. You'll find loads of tips on ingredients and equipment that will enhance your cooking experience whether you're cooking in front of a charcoal grill or an indoor stove.

If you are holding this book, you probably do not need convincing that, when it comes to grilling, there is no substitute for the flavor of charcoal grilling. Whether you are a beginner hoping to learn the charcoal ropes or a seasoned grill master looking to hone existing skills, *Kingsford Complete Grilling Cookbook* has something for you. So, fire up those grills and get cooking!

GET GRILLING

SELECTING A GRILL

You may have a big bag of briquets sitting on your deck, but they won't do you much good without a grill to hold them. Choosing a grill is like picking a new car—your choice has a lot to do with your personality and how you plan on using your purchase. Do you insist on the latest model with all of the bells and whistles, or are you returning to a familiar tried-and-true brand that you've "driven" many times before? Are you a weekend "driver," or do you plan to take long "trips"? Are you holding out for big, shiny bodywork, or would you be just as happy with a no-frills compact?

There are three basic grill designs: **kettle, brazier,** and **specialty/hybrid.** Each has passionate fans, but it is hard to argue that one is actually better than another. Regardless of the design, features to consider are ease of ash disposal, a thermometer in the lid to tell the interior temperature, the size of the cooking grate, how additional briquets are added to an existing fire, efficient air circulation (which is important to control the heat), and convenience of buying replacement parts. You don't have to depend on tire-kicking at a dealership anymore, as there are many places online that compare different brands and have owner reviews. And grills can be purchased online, too, which is helpful if you have your heart set on an obscure Grill from the Gods that can't be found at your local home and garden shop.

The **kettle grill** is probably the most familiar model. Made from sturdy metal, it has a spherical shape that reveals its original function as a buoy! Vents at the top and bottom regulate the oxygen flow, which affects the heat level of the fire—the more oxygen, the hotter the fire burns. Unlike with the brazier grill, with kettle grills, the level of the coals cannot be adjusted, so you have to learn to how to adjust the heat with the vents and the amount of charcoal to use, a skill that is not complicated and comes easily. The standard grilling grate size is 22½ inches in diameter; there are smaller 18½-inch grids and huge 37½-inch-diameter models. The standard 22½-inch kettle is the one most likely to be found in America's backyards, and it was used to test these recipes.

Brazier grills have square or rectangular grates, although their housing may be barrel-shaped. While they have vents for air control, you can easily adjust the heat with a lever or crank that raises or lowers the firebox holding the briquets. The cooking surface of these grills tends to be larger than that of the kettle grills.

Specialty/hybrid grills have features unique to their design. They often mix elements of traditional grills with those of smokers (which create smoked, and not grilled, food). The oval grill/smoker, which looks like a big ceramic or metal egg, has devoted followers. Some grills have smoke boxes off to one side of the grill to move the smoke source farther away from the food, which also reduces the heat. Smaller tabletop grills are portable and good to bring along to picnics, as long as you aren't cooking for a crowd.

ALL ABOUT CHARCOAL

Created from wood that has been heated in the absence of oxygen, with moisture removed and the wood carbonized so it burns hotter and longer, charcoal is the fuel of choice for millions of grill masters. Lump charcoal is this charred wood in its unchanged state. Some grill cooks like lump charcoal because it burns very hot. However, it also burns away relatively fast, and its irregular shape can create hot spots, so you must give the fire extra attention to address these issues.

Briquets are made of granular charcoal compressed into individual pillow shapes. Each briquet burns at the same rate, giving off reliable, steady heat. The Kingsford Products Company was the first firm to manufacture briquets commercially, and they remain the industry leader. The original "recipe" was in use for almost 90 years, but there has been a recent reformulation, Kingsford® Charcoal with Sure Fire Grooves™, that allows the briquets to ignite more quickly and burn even hotter and longer than was ordinary.

In addition to the regular briquets, Kingsford also makes Match Light® Instant Light Charcoal (for lighting without lighter fluid), Kingsford® Charcoal with Mesquite (to impart an extra layer of woody flavor to your food), and Match Light® Instant Charcoal with Mesquite. For one-time-use charcoal briquets, look for the Kingsford® BBQ Bag.

Stored in a cool, dark place, charcoal will keep indefinitely. Moisture is the enemy of charcoal—damp charcoal will not ignite. Do not use charcoal for any other use than as a cooking fuel. For household uses like absorbing odors, use activated charcoal, available at plant nurseries and pet stores. And charcoal ashes are not meant to be used as compost or fertilizer, so do not distribute them in your garden.

LIGHTING THE PERFECT FIRE

There are a number of ways to light the fire for the grill. Sure Fire Grooves™ improve the air flow around and inside the briquets, and as oxygen supply is crucial to the intensity of the flame, the briquets will be ready in about 15 minutes.

How many briquets? For a standard 22½-inch-diameter grill, use about 5 pounds briquets. Don't take out a scale—just pour the amount needed from the bag. Use about half of a 9-pound bag, a third of a 15-pound bag, or a quarter of a 21.6-pound bag.

Brazier grills have differing dimensions, so the amount of coals varies. For average use, light enough briquets to provide a double- to triple-thick layer of coals at one side of the grill, and a single-briquet depth on the other side. This "banked" grilling setup is the most versatile method. The easiest way to estimate this amount is to spread unignited charcoal in the grill in the banked pattern, taking note of the volume used. Once you know the amount of coals for this setup, you can use less for indirect heat or more for direct heat.

No matter what method you use to light the fire, let the fire burn until the charcoal is about 70 percent covered with white ash. By the time you spread it out, replace the grill grid, and do a few other steps to ready the food for the grill, the coals will be completely covered with ash, which indicates that they are at the peak of their heat curve.

Here are various ways to build a charcoal fire:

LEFT TO RIGHT: **Stack the briquets and squirt with the fluid.** ■ **Light with a long match.**
■ **Spread out the ignited coals.**

The Pyramid with Lighter Fluid. Charcoal stacked pyramid-style and ignited with the help

of lighter fluid is a time-tested method for starting the fire. It is one of the quickest methods because it exposes the maximum surface of the charcoal to fire. When used correctly, the lighter fluid aroma will burn off. Problems with lingering lighter fluid aroma and taste occur when grill cooks get anxious and apply more fluid than needed. The excess fluid splashes into the interior of the grill or into the ash can, and it is this overflow that inadvertently flavors the food.

Pour the required amount of coals (about 5 pounds for a standard kettle grill) in the center of the charcoal grate. This is the grate closest to the bottom of the grill, not to be confused with the grilling grate in the upper section of the grill, which holds the food. Stack the charcoal in a rough pyramid shape. Squirt the lighter fluid over the surface of the charcoal. You've added enough lighter fluid when the charcoal is glossy. Carefully light the charcoal with a match or "click" igniter. Do not cover the grill, as the fire needs oxygen to live. Let the fire ignite. Be patient, as it will take at least 5 minutes before you see ashes begin to form around the corners of the briquets. When the coals are almost covered with white ash, spread the coals as required for direct, indirect, banked, or pocket grilling.

LEFT TO RIGHT (FROM TOP TO BOTTOM): **Stuff chimney with two sheets of newspaper.** ■ **Light the paper.**
■ **Burn the briquets until 70 percent ashed-over.** ■ **Pour out the coals.** ■ **Spread out the ignited coals.**

The Charcoal Chimney. A tall, chimney-like canister with a large handle, this tool uses newspaper as its fuel to ignite the charcoal. Store chimneys in a dry place (not where they can get rained on), and they will last forever. To use, place the chimney on the charcoal grate. Fill the smaller bottom compartment with two double sheets of crumpled newspaper. Do not overstuff the bottom compartment, or the air flow will be impeded and the charcoal will not light. Fill the chimney just to the top with charcoal. Do not add lighter fluid or cover the grill. Light the newspaper. Because the chimney is narrower than a pyramid, it will take a bit longer for the briquets to burn until they are almost covered with white ash. Pour the charcoal out of the chimney into the required formation.

LEFT TO RIGHT: **Twist newspaper into a rope.** ■ **Tie into an overhand knot.** ■ **Place in the grill bottom.** ■ **Light the newspaper.**

The Newspaper Knot. For the most low-tech method of lighting charcoal, use newspaper. This technique could come in handy in situations where you have neither lighter fluid nor a chimney, perhaps at a park with basic grills.

Starting at a long end, twist two sheets of a newspaper double spread into a thick rope. Tie the newspaper rope in a large overhand knot. Make two or three newspaper knots. Place the newspaper knots in the bottom of the grill, then position the charcoal grate in place. Build a pyramid of charcoal, light the newspaper, and let the charcoal burn, uncovered, to the ashed-over stage.

Cube Starters. Solid starter cubes, made from petroleum or alcohol, are another way to start a fire. They release a small flame, so are slower starting than the other methods. However, the cubes are small and take up little space for storage.

Build a pyramid of charcoal in the grill. Tuck a starter cube in the bottom layer in a position that allows you to light the cube with a long match or igniter. Do not cover the grill. Let the fire burn until the coals are almost completely ashed over.

Electric Starter. The biggest caveat to this tool is that you must have an electric outlet nearby your grill in order to use it. Some starters have short cords, so have a heavy-duty extension cord, too.

Place the starter in the bottom of the charcoal grate and build a pyramid of charcoal on top. Plug in the starter to heat the charcoal to the point when the coals that come into contact with the heating element are tinged with ash, about 12 minutes. Remove the starter, stir the charcoal with long tongs to distribute the hot coals with the unlighted ones, and let the coals burn uncovered until coated with ash.

TYPES OF GRILLING

When you bake in the oven, do you use only one temperature regardless of the food? If you're cooking in a skillet on top of the stove, do you use only high heat? In both cases, it is more than likely that you will adjust the heat as needed. Then why is it that so many grill cooks think that the only way to grill food is directly over high heat? Think of your grill as an outdoor oven whose tmperature can be changed with the amount of charcoal used and how it is positioned, adjusting the air vents to control the air flow, and you'll have better grilled food.

There are four grilling methods used in this book: direct, indirect, banked, and pocket. The recipes for this book were developed with Kingsford® Charcoal Briquets with Sure Fire Grooves™. Because these new briquets burn much hotter and longer than the previous formulation, the timings and even recommended grilling methods for some of your favorite recipes may have changed. Use these recipes as guidelines and apply them to your old recipes to gauge the new cooking times.

LEFT TO RIGHT: Spread the coals to within 2 inches of grill edge. ■ Test the heat with your hand over the grate. ■ Regulate the heat with the vent.

Direct Grilling. This works best for foods that cook in less than 30 minutes over coals with hot or medium heat, including sausages, hot dogs, and most steaks. For **Direct High Grilling**, build a charcoal fire with the full amount (about 5 pounds) of charcoal. (If using a charcoal chimney, fill it to the top.) When the coals are ready, spread them in a thick layer over the charcoal grate, but leave a 2-inch-wide border around the edges. This way, if flare-ups occur, you can move the food over the empty area, where the dripping fat is less likely to ignite. Because of the density of the coals, the fire will be very hot, averaging around 550°F for at least the first 30 minutes or so.

To build a fire for **Direct Medium Grilling**, which is often used for fish, use only 3 pounds (fill a chimney half-full) of charcoal. Spread the ashed-over coals in a thin layer over the charcoal grate. Let the fire burn until you can hold your hand over the coals for about 3 seconds—this should take about 10 minutes. If you want to grill immediately, without waiting for the coals to cool, adjust the vents to half-closed.

Direct Low Grilling is rarely utilized, but it can be useful if you want to warm up some fruit for dessert over the almost-spent coals from a main course. In this case, simply let the coals burn down until you can hold your hand over them for about 5 seconds.

Indirect Grilling. With this method, the food is cooked by the indirect radiant heat of the coals. It is ideal for foods that are higher in fat or those that are best cooked in a way similar to oven roasting—chicken, beef brisket and roasts, pork roasts and spareribs, even desserts. It usually uses low or moderate heat and is often combined with smoke from soaked wood chips to simulate the flavor of slow-cooked barbecue. A drip pan is usually placed under the food to catch dripping fat. This is the method used for long-cooked foods, and you may have to add additional charcoal as the fire burns down.

To prepare a grill for Indirect Grilling, use only 3 pounds of briquets. This reduced amount of charcoal will help achieve a lower interior grill temperature. When the coals are ready, heap them on one side of the grill, leaving the other side empty. Some grill cooks prefer to make two heaps, one on either side of the grill, to give two sources of heat. However, this reduces the cooking area and means that when the coals burn down and need stoking, you will have to add fresh briquets to both sides instead of to one. The one-sided method works well in a kettle grill, the design of which encourages excellent air flow to surround the food with heat. Under most circumstances, you won't usually have to turn the food to give equal exposure to the heat. In brazier grills with large cooking grates, the two-sided approach might be better.

Place a disposable aluminum foil pan, about 13 × 9-inches, in the empty area of the grill. If you grill a lot, buy a stack of these pans so you won't run out. Do not use baking pans from your kitchen, as they will eventually discolor from the heat and smoke of the grill. You can wash the disposable foil pans and reuse them quite a few times before they wear out. In a pinch, create an impromptu drip pan by molding a large, double-thick sheet of aluminum foil over an inverted 13 × 9-inch metal or glass baking pan and lifting the molded foil away.

Pour about 2 cups of water in the pan. You can use beer, wine, or diluted juice as the liquid, but these really only give off their aroma, and add very little, if any, actual flavor to

LEFT TO RIGHT (FROM TOP TO BOTTOM): Build the fire with 3 pounds of briquets. ■ Pour the coals on one side of the grill. ■ With the drip pan on the empty side, pour water into pan. ■ Sprinkle soaked chips over the coals. ■ Occasionally add fresh briquets to the fire. ■ Test the heat with a meat thermometer in the lid vent.

the food. The water will catch and dilute dripping fat that would otherwise burn in the hot pan, and will create some steam to help dissolve fat. Usually, the water does not need to be replenished, but do so if it evaporates. Place the food over the pan and cover the grill.

To regulate the temperature in the grill, adjust the vents in the top and bottom to half-open. Allow the temperature to stabilize, then check with a thermometer (see "Temperature Control," page 12). If needed, add a few more coals or open or close the vents to achieve an average temperature of 275° to 325°F for **Indirect Low Grilling**, and 350° to 400°F for **Indirect Medium Grilling**. If the coals fall below the lower end of the scale, add 8 to 12 unlighted briquets to the coals, and replace the grill cover. The coals will ignite more slowly than if the lid were open. If the recipe calls for wood chips, sprinkle them over the coals first, then add the fresh charcoal.

With **Indirect High Heat**, used for whole chickens and beef or pork roasts, the temperature will start out high (about 550°F) and slowly drop to about 350°F over a period of 1½ hours. The coals that are added are used to keep the temperature from dropping below 350°F, not to bring it back up to its initial starting point. After adding the food to the grill, cover and leave the vents wide open so the fire initially burns hot.

LEFT TO RIGHT: **Spread the coals into high and low heat areas.** ■ **Sear the meat over the high area, then move to low.**

Banked Grilling. This is the most useful method, for it allows for two zones of high and moderate heat, which give more options than either direct or indirect grilling. It is especially useful for foods like thick steaks and boneless chicken breasts, where you want to develop a deeply browned exterior, but need gentler heat to cook the meat through without drying out. The food is seared to begin the browning process over the high coals, and moved to the cooler area to finish cooking. Or the food is cooked directly over the cooler coals without searing, with additional heat radiating from the hotter bank.

DEALING WITH FLARE-UPS (NOT)

Flare-ups are the bane of the grill master. They are caused by fat or oil dripping from the food onto the coals. If the grill is uncovered, and the flames are fed with oxygen, the fire will burn ever hotter. There are two easy solutions. First, set up the coals so there are empty areas to move the dripping food away from direct contact with the heat. Second, covering the grill during cooking reduces the oxygen, and keeps flare-ups in check. If you always take these two steps, your flare-up problems will disappear. As a last resort, extinguish stubborn flare-ups with a squirt of water from a spray bottle, taking care not to splash ashes all over the food. This is only a temporary fix, and until you repair the source of the flare-up by moving the food or reducing the oxygen, the flames will come back.

Build the fire with 5 pounds of charcoal. Spread the charcoal (or pour, if using a chimney starter) in a bank in the bottom of the grill, with a double- to triple-thick layer on one side of the grill and a single layer of coals on the other side.

Pocket Grilling. Use this method to surround burgers with high heat while providing an empty space underneath each patty to drip fat and avoid flare-ups. Build a fire with 5 pounds of charcoal. When they are almost covered with ash, use long tongs to dig one pocket in the coals for each burger. The burgers are seared over the coals, then moved to over the pockets and covered to complete cooking.

LEFT TO RIGHT: **Make pockets in the coals with tongs. ■ Cook the burgers over the pocketed areas.**

GRILLING BASICS

Meat and poultry will grill more evenly if it isn't chilled. In these recipes, we recommend seasoning the food, then letting it stand at room temperature while the fire is heating up. If you have the time, let the food stand for at least 1 and up to 2 hours.

Once you've determined how the food will be grilled, prepare the cooking grate. Always discard any residual ashes in the grill before cooking. A thick layer of ashes will act as insulation, affecting the distribution of heat and air circulation. Now you can build your fire according to your preferred method.

When the fire is ready, spread the coals as desired and replace the cooking grate. Scrub the grate well with a long-handled stiff wire grill brush to remove any residual food. If the grill was cleaned right after the previous grilling session, as it should be, there will be very little residue. To keep the food from sticking to the grill, lightly oil the grill with a thick, rolled-up cylinder of paper towels dipped in flavorless vegetable oil. If you use an oil spray, remove the grate from the grill, spray it well away from the coals, and return it to the grill. Look for oil sprays that are specifically formulated for the high temperature of grills. Never spray directly onto the coals. In some cases, as with fish, the food is lightly oiled, too, to discourage sticking.

Let the grate heat for a few minutes until it is very hot. This will make distinct grill marks on the food.

Place the food on the grill, leaving space around each food item to allow for even cooking and heat penetration. Now cover the grill. Adjust the vents as needed, leaving them open for a hot fire or partially closed for a lower heat. There is some disagreement about whether to grill with the lid on or off. Some grill cooks feel that you can taste the interior of the grill, but they must be cooking in dirty grills. With the lid on, the heat is trapped under the cover and the food cooks more quickly. In addition, oxygen flow is reduced, cutting down on flare-ups, and as a bonus, your food will acquire a smokier flavor. During cooking, keep the lid on as much as possible, because every time the lid is opened, heat will escape.

Don't turn the food too often during grilling, as you could inadvertently force moisture out of it. Allowing the food to brown before turning develops the flavorful crust that is the signature of great grilling. Use tongs or a spatula for turning, as a fork could pierce the food and release juices. Apply sauces containing sugar, honey, or molasses no sooner than the last 10 minutes of cooking to prevent the sauce from burning. After the food is cooked, get in the habit of brushing the grilling grate while the food residue is still hot. This will remove the residue before it has a chance to burn onto the grate.

TEMPERATURE CONTROL

You can control the interior temperature of your grill by adjusting the grill vents, and by the amount of charcoal used. But it is helpful to have actual target temperatures.

High	**475° to 600°F**
Medium-high	**400° to 475°F**
Medium	**325° to 400°F**
Low	**275° to 325°F**

The best way to check the temperature is with a thermometer. You will be especially glad that you used a thermometer with long-cooked foods like brisket or pork shoulder, as it can be a bit of a challenge to maintain steady temperatures over a long period of time.

Some grills come with thermometers installed in their lids, which show the temperature without your having to open the lid and lose heat. If you don't have a built-in thermometer, use a food or deep-frying thermometer with a long metal stem that reaches up to 550°F. Drop the thermometer stem through the lid vent to get the reading. It can stay in place throughout grilling. If you use a grill thermometer that sits directly on the grill grate, open and close the lid quickly to read the dial to keep heat from escaping.

The "hand test" is another way for gauging the grill temperature, and works best with direct heat grilling. With the coals ignited and in their proper position for the chosen grilling method, hold your hand about 1 inch above the grilling grate. If you can hold it at that position for only 1 second, the coals are at high heat; at 2 seconds, the coals are medium-high; 3 seconds for medium; and at 4 to 5 seconds, the coals are low.

Remember that the weather will affect how hot the fire burns. If the weather is cool and breezy, compensate by using extra charcoal to build up the heat.

WHEN IS IT DONE?

The USDA recommends temperatures for cooked foods that destroy harmful bacteria. In most cases, the food will be well-done. If you choose to cook your food to lower temperatures than the USDA recommendations, there is some risk involved. In this book, we use temperatures that show the food to its best culinary advantage, often medium-rare. It is a simple matter to cook food longer, if you wish, but once meat, poultry, or seafood is cooked to well-done, there is no turning back.

A food thermometer is a fine way to check the doneness of food, and an instant-read thermometer gives the fastest results. Probe-stemmed models with digital readouts let the cook monitor the progress of the food as it cooks. There are even remote models so you can carry the readout unit with you. Insert the stem in the center of the food for the most accurate reading. When the thermometer won't stand in thin steaks and chops, insert it horizontally through the side at the center of the meat. Never leave a dial-headed instant-read thermometer in the food, as the plastic dome covering the dial will melt. Even with probe-style digital thermometers, be sure that the model you have can withstand the high heat of the grill—some are meant for oven use only.

Thermometers are fast and accurate, but they aren't the only way to test food. You should learn to use your senses of sight and touch to judge doneness, too. For example, when cooking a steak, you'll see tiny drops of red juice appear on the top surface when the meat is ready to be turned (if you are going for medium-rare meat). Seafood changes from translucent to opaque, and shrimp will have streaks of orange or dark pink.

When meat and poultry cook, juices evaporate, and the flesh gets firmer. Press the food in its thickest part to assess the doneness by touch. Medium-rare meat will feel somewhat firm. Medium meat will be resilient, with some "give." Well-done meat will feel quite firm and will spring back.

Before slicing meat or poultry, let it stand on a carving board for at least 5 minutes. This allows the juices in the meat to retract back into the flesh. Large cuts of meat, such as brisket and prime rib, and turkeys can stand for 20 minutes or so without cooling too much. The extra resting time will only increase their juiciness.

Take "carry-over" cooking into consideration, too. When cooked meat or poultry is removed from the cooking source (be it a grill or an oven), it retains heat, and the internal temperature of the food will continue to rise for a few minutes by a couple of degrees before beginning the cooling process. The larger the item, the more dramatic the temperature rise—you can expect a carry-over of 5° to 10°F with big turkeys and beef rib roasts, but less with smaller roasts, steaks, and chops. The recommended temperatures and timings in this book take the carry-over cooking into account.

FINISHING UP

Brush the grill grate clean. Cover the grill and close all the vents. Allow the coals to burn out completely. Let the ashes cool for 48 hours before disposing of them in a noncombustible container.

If you must dispose of coals before they've completely cooled, remove them with long-handled tongs and carefully bury them in a can of sand or dirt. Never use water to extinguish coals, as the hot steam could burn you.

SAFE GRILLING

Start with choosing a safe location for the grill—a flat, level surface where it won't tip over. Keep the grill away from fences, deck railings, and shrubbery that could be ignited by a sudden flare-up.

Use the grill in a well-ventilated location. Never grill indoors, as toxic carbon monoxide can build up. And keep the kids and pets away from the grill when it's in use. Handle charcoal carefully. Never add lighter fluid to a sluggish fire to get it going again. If coals are

WOOD PRODUCTS FOR GRILLING

Aromatic wood chips, chunks, and planks add an extra layer of smoky flavor to food. The chips are easy to use because they begin to smolder almost immediately when tossed on the coals. Some grill cooks like the large wood chunks, but they take extra time to soak. Briquets embedded with mesquite chips are easiest of all.

The two most popular woods are mesquite and hickory, both native American varieties that can lend their sweet smokiness to a wide range of foods. The former is especially tasty with beef, chicken, and salmon, and the latter partners beautifully with pork and chicken. Oak and grape match well with wine-marinated meats and poultry. Fruit woods, such as cherry, apple, or peach, and pecan go with fruit-glazed meats. Maple, alder, and cedar planks are great with salmon and other fish.

These wood products for grilling are always soaked in cold water to cover before using. Give them at least 30 minutes to rehydrate. Longer is fine, but don't let them stand in water for longer than 8 hours, or they could develop an off flavor. Drain the wood just before using, but don't bother with draining in a strainer. Just grab a handful of chips and let the excess water run through your fingers. Toss the chips on the coals, and you're in business. For long-cooked foods, add more chips every hour or whenever you add more fresh briquets to the grill. If you grill often with wood chips, as a smart time-saver, freeze the soaked and drained chips in plastic bags, and use these chilly chips without soaking again.

slow to start, place several new briquets in a small metal can and add lighter fluid. Using long-handled tongs, add the new soaked briquets to the warm coals and ignite with a match. Never use gas or kerosene to light a charcoal fire, as both can cause an explosion.

Remember that coals are extremely hot—they can reach up to 1500°F—so treat them with respect. Use insulated, preferably flame-retardant gloves when handling any part of a hot grill. Use long-handled tongs for safe handling of food and coals.

Keep your grill clean! Every 3 months or so, give it a thorough scrub-down with grill cleaner (there are many such products on the market), oven cleaner, or just some detergent and elbow grease. This keeps ashes and rendered cooking fats, both of which will affect the flavor of your food, from building up inside of the grill. Don't forget to wash the interior of the lid, too. If you see black flakes on the inside of the lid, it is buildup, not paint, but should be removed anyway.

THE HISTORY OF KINGSFORD

The cast of characters in the development of the charcoal briquet includes a university professor, automotive genius Henry Ford, inventor Thomas Edison, and an automobile salesman.

The saga starts with Orin Stafford, a University of Oregon professor who was looking to devise commercially viable charcoal from wood waste material. His experiments led him to a special process that bound granular charred wood into pillow-shaped briquets.

Henry Ford was eager to find a way to use up the leftover wood that piled up from the manufacturing of Model Ts. He learned of Stafford's process and worked with Thomas Edison to design a charcoal plant in Iron Mountain, Michigan, where the sawmill for Ford's cars was located. The superintendent of the plant was E. G. Kingsford, a relative of Ford's who owned one of the first Ford sales agencies.

By the end of 1924, the plant was producing 55 tons of briquets each day, which were originally sold to such industries as meat and fish smokehouses. Later, a worker at the plant got the bright idea that the briquets would make quick and easy campfires. The briquets were packaged in bags, emblazoned with the Ford logo, and sold with inexpensive outdoor grills. A company town was built near the plant and christened "Kingsford." Now the name Kingsford is synonymous with grilling.

ESSENTIAL GRILLING EQUIPMENT

SPRING-LOADED TONGS. Use long tongs to turn and move food on the grill. Spring-loaded tongs with blunt ends have the firmest grip. Never use a meat fork to turn grilled food, as it will pierce the food and release juices.

LONG TONGS FOR CHARCOAL. To move charcoal, reserve a second pair of long metal tongs—the ones used to reach items on a tall shelf are ideal.

SPATULA. A thin, but relatively wide, metal spatula with a long handle will make easy work of turning burgers.

WIRE BRUSH. Get a long-handled, sturdy wire grilling brush to scrub the cooking grate clean. A scraper at the end will help remove tough spots.

CARVING BOARD. A wooden or plastic carving board with a well collects the juices from carving and helps keep them off of the kitchen counter.

METAL SKEWERS. Long metal, flat-bladed skewers hold food for grilling.

WOODEN SKEWERS. Soaked and drained, these are used when the food will be grilled in a short period of time. Thin bamboo sticks are common, but look for thicker wooden skewers that will hold up to heat.

BASTING BRUSH. While natural bristle brushes are fine, a silicone brush is easier to clean and won't soak up liquids.

ASSORTED GRILL BASKETS. You'll find wire mesh baskets specifically designed to hold whole fish. An adjustable grill basket can hold kebabs, fish fillets, and other foods.

GRILLING GRATE. This flat, perforated metal plate can be placed on the cooking grid to keep small pieces of food from falling into the coals.

INSTANT-READ THERMOMETER. A stemmed instant-read thermometer or a probe-style digital thermometer (get one specifically for grilling) gives fast, accurate readings.

ELECTRIC SPICE GRINDER/MORTAR AND PESTLE. These grind spices and herbs for spice rubs.

ALUMINUM FOIL DRIP PANS. With indirect grilling (see page 8), these are placed under the food to catch dripping fat.

CHIMNEY STARTER. Uses newspaper to ignite charcoal.

MITTS. Flame-retardant fireplace gloves are great to use with the high heat from a grill, but heavy quilted oven mitts work well, too.

SAUCES, RUBS, MARINADES, AND BRINES

ALL-AMERICAN BARBECUE SAUCE

GRILLING CLASSIC

MAKES ABOUT 4 CUPS

When you feel like mixing up a batch of your own barbecue sauce, you can't go wrong with this one, which is everything people expect. It's **tangy, sweet, and zippy,** and goes great with **everything from ribs to steaks to chicken.** You may as well make a double batch, because it lasts for a long time in the refrigerator. And try one of the variations, which bring the distinctive flavors of maple and apple to the table.

2 TABLESPOONS VEGETABLE OIL

1 LARGE ONION, FINELY CHOPPED

2 GARLIC CLOVES, FINELY CHOPPED

1 CUP KETCHUP-STYLE CHILI SAUCE

1 CUP TOMATO KETCHUP

1/2 CUP CIDER VINEGAR

1/2 CUP UNSULFURED MOLASSES

2 TABLESPOONS SPICY BROWN OR DIJON MUSTARD

2 TABLESPOONS WORCESTERSHIRE SAUCE

2 TABLESPOONS STEAK SAUCE (OPTIONAL)

HOT RED PEPPER SAUCE TO TASTE

1. Heat the oil in a heavy-bottomed medium saucepan over medium heat. Add the onion and cook, stirring occasionally, until golden, about 8 minutes. Stir in the garlic and cook until fragrant, about 1 minute.

2. Add the chili sauce, ketchup, vinegar, molasses, mustard, Worcestershire sauce, and steak sauce, if using. Bring to a simmer and reduce the heat to medium-low. Simmer, stirring often to be sure the sauce isn't sticking, until slightly reduced, about 20 minutes. Stir in the hot pepper sauce. Transfer to a bowl and cool. (The sauce can be made up to 6 weeks ahead, cooled, stored in an airtight container, and refrigerated.)

VARIATIONS:

Yankee Maple Barbecue Sauce: Substitute 1/2 cup maple-flavored pancake syrup for the molasses. If you want to use pure maple syrup, use Grade B (which has a deeper flavor than Grade A) and 1/2 teaspoon pure maple extract to the finished sauce.

Big Apple Barbecue Sauce: Substitute 2/3 cup apple butter for the molasses.

ATLANTA BARBECUE SAUCE

MAKES ABOUT 4 CUPS

Peaches and cola soda, whether from Georgia or not, give **fruity notes** to this sauce. Your **pork chops** and **chicken** will love you for it, especially when grilled with hickory wood chips.

2 TABLESPOONS VEGETABLE OIL

1 LARGE SWEET ONION, SUCH AS VIDALIA, FINELY CHOPPED

2 GARLIC CLOVES, FINELY CHOPPED

2 CUPS TOMATO KETCHUP

1/2 CUP CARBONATED COLA BEVERAGE

1/2 CUP PEACH PRESERVES

1/3 CUP FRESH LEMON JUICE

2 TABLESPOONS SPICY BROWN OR DIJON MUSTARD

1/2 TEASPOON CRUSHED HOT RED PEPPER

HOT RED PEPPER SAUCE TO TASTE

1. Heat the oil in a heavy-bottomed medium saucepan over medium heat. Add the onion and cover. Cook, stirring occasionally, until tender, about 10 minutes. Stir in the garlic and cook until fragrant, about 1 minute.

2. Add the ketchup, cola, peach preserves, lemon juice, mustard, and hot pepper and bring to a simmer. Reduce the heat to medium-low. Simmer, uncovered, stirring often to be sure the sauce isn't sticking, until reduced by about one-fourth, about 30 minutes. Stir in the hot pepper sauce. Transfer to a bowl and cool. (The sauce can be made up to 6 weeks ahead, cooled, stored in an airtight container, and refrigerated.)

USING BARBECUE SAUCES

When you find a barbecue sauce you like, there is temptation to slather it on everything, and maybe even use it as a marinade. If your taste buds allow, you can do the first thing, but hold off on the second, even if Dad taught you otherwise.

There is one important trick to using barbecue sauce. Because most of the sauces have a fair amount of sugar, they can burn easily when exposed to the heat of a charcoal grill. So, do not brush your grilled food with barbecue sauce until the last few minutes of grilling, or your favorite sauce could literally burn to a crisp.

SANTA ROSA BARBECUE SAUCE

Santa Rosa, California, was once home to botanist Luther Burbank, who did a lot to improve **apricots** and bring them to market across the nation. To give your grilled **spareribs** a real treat, use this sauce.

2 TABLESPOONS VEGETABLE OIL

6 SCALLIONS, WHITE AND GREEN PARTS, FINELY CHOPPED

2 TABLESPOONS SHREDDED FRESH GINGER (USE THE LARGE HOLES ON A BOX GRATER)

1/2 JALAPEÑO, SEEDED AND MINCED

2 GARLIC CLOVES, FINELY CHOPPED

2 CUPS TOMATO KETCHUP

1/2 CUP APRICOT PRESERVES

1/2 CUP WHITE WINE VINEGAR

2 TABLESPOONS WHOLE GRAIN MUSTARD

2 TABLESPOONS SOY SAUCE

1. Heat the oil in a heavy-bottomed medium saucepan over medium heat. Add the scallions, ginger, jalapeño, and garlic and cook, stirring often, until the scallions soften, about 1 minute.

2. Add the ketchup, apricot preserves, vinegar, mustard, and soy sauce. Bring to a simmer and reduce the heat to medium-low. Simmer, stirring often to be sure the sauce isn't sticking, until slightly reduced, about 20 minutes. Transfer to a bowl and cool. (The sauce can be made up to 6 weeks ahead, cooled, stored in an airtight container, and refrigerated.)

FRESH GINGER

Store a big knob of fresh ginger in your refrigerator's produce drawer to have ready for adding zesty, spicy flavor to your cooking. Wrapped in aluminum foil, it will last for a week or two. Many recipes call for mincing peeled fresh ginger, but shredding on the large holes of a box grater speeds this chore along. And while it's a nicety to remove the think ginger skin with a vegetable peeler, it really isn't imperative, unless the peel's dark beige color will affect the appearance of the dish. Fresh ginger juice, easily extracted by squeezing freshly shredded ginger in your fist, is an especially effective way to get ginger's pungent taste in your food while bypassing its rough texture.

ORANGE-CHIPOTLE BARBECUE SAUCE

MAKES ABOUT 4 CUPS

The combination of orange and chiles seems to bring out the best in both ingredients, so why not make the flavors as intense as possible? Orange juice concentrate is about as **orange-y** as you can get, and the same can be said for the **spicy-smoky** qualities found in chipotle chiles. Here's another sauce that is compatible with **pork and chicken,** and it also works as a glaze on **salmon fillets.**

2 TABLESPOONS VEGETABLE OIL

1 LARGE ONION, CHOPPED

2 GARLIC CLOVES, FINELY CHOPPED

1 CUP TOMATO KETCHUP

1 CUP KETCHUP-STYLE CHILI SAUCE

1/2 CUP PACKED LIGHT BROWN SUGAR

1/3 CUP FROZEN ORANGE JUICE CONCENTRATE (SEE NOTE)

2 CANNED CHIPOTLE CHILES IN ADOBO, WITH ANY CLINGING SAUCE, MINCED

GRATED ZEST OF 1 LARGE ORANGE

1. Heat the oil in a heavy-bottomed medium saucepan over medium heat. Add the onion and cook, stirring occasionally, until golden, about 8 minutes. Stir in the garlic and cook until fragrant, about 1 minute.

2. Add the ketchup, chili sauce, brown sugar, orange juice concentrate, and chipotle. Bring to a simmer and reduce the heat to medium-low. Simmer, stirring often to be sure the sauce isn't sticking, until slightly reduced, about 20 minutes. Stir in the orange zest. Transfer to a bowl and cool. (The sauce can be made up to 6 weeks ahead, cooled, stored in an airtight container, and refrigerated.)

Note: This is the frozen cylinder of concentrated juice that many people reconstitute with water to make their morning juice. Just scrape off what you need from the top of the frozen juice. If you reconstitute the remaining juice for a beverage, just use about ½ can less water than called for in the instructions.

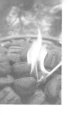

SEATTLE BARBECUE SAUCE

The culture and cuisine of Seattle has **many Asian influences.** This barbecue sauce does, too, with hoisin sauce, ginger, rice vinegar, and Asian hot sauce mixing it up. Spread it on **salmon steaks, pork tenderloins, or flank steaks.**

2 TABLESPOONS VEGETABLE OIL

4 SCALLIONS, WHITE AND GREEN PARTS, FINELY CHOPPED

2 TABLESPOONS SHREDDED FRESH GINGER (USE THE LARGE HOLES ON A BOX GRATER)

2 GARLIC CLOVES, FINELY CHOPPED

2 CUPS TOMATO KETCHUP

⅓ CUP RICE VINEGAR

½ CUP HOISIN SAUCE

2 TABLESPOONS CHINESE RICE WINE OR DRY SHERRY

1 TEASPOON ASIAN HOT SAUCE, SUCH AS SRIRACHA, OR HOT RED PEPPER SAUCE

1. Heat the oil in a heavy-bottomed medium saucepan over medium heat. Add the scallions, ginger, and garlic and cook, stirring often, until the scallions soften, about 1 minute.

2. Stir in the ketchup, vinegar, hoisin sauce, and rice wine and bring to a simmer. Reduce the heat to medium-low. Simmer, stirring often to be sure the sauce isn't sticking, until slightly reduced, about 20 minutes. Stir in the Asian hot sauce. Transfer to a bowl and cool. (The sauce can be made up to 6 weeks ahead, cooled, stored in an airtight container, and refrigerated.)

HERBED RED WINE MARINADE

MAKES ABOUT 2 CUPS, ENOUGH FOR UP TO 5 POUNDS OF MEAT

This **aromatic, robust marinade** will add an extra dimension of flavor to red meats. Use a full-bodied, not-too-fruity red wine as the base—a Cabernet-Shiraz blend is a good choice, particularly one that hasn't been oaked. Try this with **leg of lamb, lamb kebabs, flank steak, or beef tenderloin.**

1 CUP HEARTY RED WINE, SUCH AS CABERNET-SHIRAZ BLEND

1/3 CUP EXTRA-VIRGIN OLIVE OIL

1/4 CUP BALSAMIC VINEGAR

2 TABLESPOONS SOY SAUCE

1 TABLESPOON HERBES DE PROVENCE, OR 1 TEASPOON EACH DRIED THYME, ROSEMARY, AND OREGANO

2 GARLIC CLOVES, CHOPPED

1 BAY LEAF

1/2 TEASPOON FRESHLY GROUND BLACK PEPPER

Whisk all of the ingredients in a medium bowl until combined. Use immediately.

- One of the essential elements of grilling, marinades have long been valued for adding flavor to grilled foods. However, recent studies show that marinating food before grilling also helps discourage by about 90 percent the formation of potentially harmful compounds that can occur from grilling. Even a brief marination will help.

- Oil from marinade dripping onto coals will ignite and irritate the grill cook trying to keep flare-ups at bay. To keep flare-ups to a minimum, keep the amount of oil in marinades to a minimum, as well. Some oil is needed to lubricate the meat so it doesn't stick to the grill grate, and if you use oil with flavor, such as olive oil, it adds taste. Otherwise, when it comes to oil in marinades, less is more.

- Marinating does *not* tenderize meats. Repeat: Marinating does *not* tenderize meats. In fact, an over-long marination (more than 8 hours) will only make the surface of the meat or poultry mushy—which is *not* tenderizing. It is much better to marinate the food in a full-flavored marinade for a shorter period of time. You will get plenty of flavor if you allow the food to marinate at room temperature while the coals ignite, or for a maximum of 2 hours. For longer periods, refrigerate the marinating food. Never marinate seafood for longer than 30 minutes under any circumstances, as the acids in the marinade will "cook" the food, similar to the effect of citrus juice in seviche.

- While you can marinate the food in a bowl or shallow dish, a 1-gallon resealable plastic bag does an even better job. The food does not have to be submerged in the marinade; as long as the marinade is touching the food, it will do its work. The plastic bag makes this possible without using excess marinade. If you prefer to use a bowl or dish, be sure that it is nonreactive (i.e., will not react with the acids in the marinade). Tempered glass and stainless steel containers are both fine, but do not use hard plastic or rubber, as it may pick up the flavor of the marinade.

- You can baste food with the reserved marinade if you do so during the first few minutes of grilling, as the marinade will be thoroughly cooked that way. However, to avoid cross-contamination from a marinade that has touched raw meat or poultry, it is better to make a double batch of the marinade and set half aside for the sole purpose of basting. These marinade recipes are so full-flavored that you won't really need the extra basting. Besides, basting can make more problems than it's worth, as the dripping marinade can kick up ashes and make flare-ups.

HERBED WHITE WINE MARINADE

Use this marinade when you want to add a **fragrant, light note** to **chicken, pork, veal, and seafood.** An unoaked, crisp, and dry white wine, such as Pinot Grigio, will work well.

1 1/2 CUPS DRY WHITE WINE, SUCH AS PINOT GRIGIO

GRATED ZEST OF 1 LEMON

1/3 CUP FRESH LEMON JUICE

1/3 CUP EXTRA-VIRGIN OLIVE OIL

2 TABLESPOONS DIJON MUSTARD

1 TABLESPOON HERBES DE PROVENCE, OR 1 TEASPOON EACH DRIED THYME, ROSEMARY, AND OREGANO

1 TEASPOON SALT

2 GARLIC CLOVES, CRUSHED UNDER A KNIFE AND PEELED

1/2 TEASPOON CRUSHED HOT RED PEPPER FLAKES

Whisk all of the ingredients in a medium bowl until combined. Use immediately.

CUBAN CITRUS MARINADE

MAKES ABOUT 2 CUPS, ENOUGH FOR UP TO 5 POUNDS OF MEAT OR POULTRY

All over the Caribbean you'll find marinades like this one, **redolent with citrus, garlic, and spices.** The rum acts as a kind of culinary solvent, releasing extra flavor for the ingredients. This is incredible with **pork,** but don't forget it when you need an interesting marinade for **chicken.**

GRATED ZEST OF 1 LARGE ORANGE

$1/2$ CUP FRESH ORANGE JUICE

GRATED ZEST OF 1 LIME

$1/2$ CUP FRESH LIME JUICE

$1/4$ CUP DARK RUM

1 TEASPOON SALT

$1/2$ TEASPOON COARSELY GROUND BLACK PEPPER (CRUSH IN A MORTAR, GRIND IN A SPICE GRINDER, OR CRUSH UNDER A HEAVY SKILLET ON A WORK SURFACE)

$1/2$ CUP EXTRA-VIRGIN OLIVE OIL

2 SCALLIONS, WHITE AND GREEN PARTS, FINELY CHOPPED

4 GARLIC CLOVES, FINELY CHOPPED

2 TEASPOONS GROUND CUMIN

2 TEASPOONS DRIED OREGANO

2 BAY LEAVES

Whisk the orange zest and juice, lime zest and juice, rum, salt, and pepper in a medium bowl. Gradually whisk in the oil. Stir in the scallions, garlic, cumin, oregano, and bay leaves. Use immediately.

MINTED YOGURT MARINADE

MAKES ABOUT 2 CUPS, ENOUGH FOR UP TO 5 POUNDS OF MEAT OR POULTRY

In this marinade, the acids in yogurt help to tenderize the meat, while infusing it with the Middle Eastern flavors of **cumin, garlic, and mint. Lamb** is a natural for this marinade, with **pork and chicken** following right behind.

2 TEASPOONS CUMIN SEEDS

2 CUPS PLAIN YOGURT

1/3 CUP CHOPPED FRESH MINT

4 GARLIC CLOVES, CRUSHED THROUGH A PRESS

1 TEASPOON SALT

1/2 TEASPOON CRUSHED HOT RED PEPPER FLAKES

1. Heat an empty small skillet over medium heat. Have a lid handy. Add the cumin seeds. Cook, stirring occasionally, until the seeds are aromatic and toasted (you may see a wisp of smoke), about 2 minutes. If the spices jump out of the pan when heating, cover the skillet with the lid.

2. Transfer the cumin to an electric spice grinder or a mortar and pestle and cool. Grind the toasted spices coarsely. Transfer to a medium bowl. Add the yogurt, mint, garlic, salt, and red pepper and mix. Use immediately.

CURRY MARINADE

Ground onions and garlic spread their flavor throughout this spicy marinade, perfect for cut-up **chicken or beef or chicken kebabs.** Madras-style curry is the most common type of the **Indian spice blend,** and the one you are likely to find at a supermarket.

2 GARLIC CLOVES, CRUSHED UNDER A KNIFE AND PEELED

SIX $\frac{1}{8}$-INCH-THICK SLICES FRESH GINGER

1 MEDIUM ONION, COARSELY CHOPPED

1$\frac{1}{2}$ CUPS PLAIN YOGURT

$\frac{1}{4}$ CUP FRESH LEMON JUICE

1 TABLESPOON MADRAS-STYLE CURRY POWDER

1 TEASPOON SALT

$\frac{1}{4}$ TEASPOON CAYENNE PEPPER

With the machine running, drop the garlic and ginger through the feed tube of a food processor fitted with the metal chopping blade to mince them. Add the onion and pulse until finely chopped. Add the yogurt, lemon juice, curry powder, salt, and cayenne and process until the marinade is smooth. (The marinade can also be made in a blender.) Use immediately.

TERIYAKI MARINADE

The **salty-sweet flavor** of teriyaki has made it one of the most **popular** of all grilling marinades. Teriyaki is a combination of two Japanese words, *teri* and *yaki,* which respectively mean luster and grill. It is sweetness that supplies the shiny look, which in a true teriyaki marinade is supplied not by sugar but by mirin, a sweetened rice wine. Try this on **chicken or beef.**

¾ CUP MIRIN

¾ CUP SOY SAUCE

3 TABLESPOONS SHREDDED FRESH GINGER (USE THE LARGE HOLES ON A BOX GRATER)

¾ TEASPOON CRUSHED HOT RED PEPPER FLAKES

3 TABLESPOONS ASIAN DARK SESAME OIL

3 GARLIC CLOVES, CHOPPED

Mix all of the ingredients in a medium bowl. Use immediately.

MIRIN

Although mirin is a rice wine, it is heavily sweetened, and used only for cooking. Therefore, it is found at Asian grocers and many supermarkets, and not liquor stores. Do not confuse it with Chinese rice wine or Japanese sake. If you can't locate it, substitute ½ cup dry sherry or bourbon and ¼ cup packed light brown sugar.

KOREAN MARINADE

The secret is in the marinade, which should include grated Asian pear or under-ripe kiwi, either of which may have enzymes that help tenderize the meat—in any case, either supplies a definite **delectable fruitiness.**

- 1 CUP SOY SAUCE
- 1 CUP DRY SHERRY
- 6 SCALLIONS, WHITE AND GREEN PARTS, CHOPPED
- 2 ASIAN PEARS, UNPEELED AND SHREDDED, OR 3 UNDER-RIPE KIWI, PEELED AND SHREDDED (USE THE LARGE HOLES OF A BOX GRATER)
- ½ CUP SUGAR
- 3 TABLESPOONS ASIAN DARK SESAME OIL
- 3 TABLESPOONS PEELED AND SHREDDED FRESH GINGER (USE THE LARGE HOLES OF A BOX GRATER)
- 6 GARLIC CLOVES, CHOPPED
- 2 TEASPOONS SESAME SEEDS
- 1 TEASPOON CRUSHED HOT RED PEPPER

Mix all of the ingredients in a medium bowl. Use immediately.

POMEGRANATE MARINADE

Until recently, the only way to get pomegranate juice was to cut one open and ream it on a juicer. Now (and your kitchen walls will be happy to hear this, too) you can get it bottled. Check the label to be sure that you are getting pomegranate juice without any other flavorings like passion fruit. This deliciously tart beverage can be used to make a **great marinade for lamb.**

- ¾ CUP BOTTLED POMEGRANATE JUICE
- ¾ CUP HEARTY RED WINE, SUCH AS CABERNET-SHIRAZ BLEND
- 2 TABLESPOONS CHOPPED FRESH PARSLEY
- 1 TEASPOON DRIED OREGANO
- 1 TEASPOON GROUND CUMIN
- 2 GARLIC CLOVES, CHOPPED
- ½ TEASPOON SALT
- ½ TEASPOON FRESHLY GROUND BLACK PEPPER
- ⅓ CUP EXTRA-VIRGIN OLIVE OIL

Whisk the juice, wine, parsley, oregano, cumin, garlic, salt, and pepper in a medium bowl. Gradually whisk in the oil. Use immediately.

STEAKHOUSE RUB

MAKES ABOUT 3 TABLESPOONS, ENOUGH FOR 4 POUNDS OF MEAT

You'll also find this **aromatic, flavorful spice crust** in the New York Strip Steaks with Steakhouse Rub on page 72, but it bears repeating here because it could become a staple in your arsenal of spice rubs. This rub, combined with the flavor of charcoal from the grill, will **elevate your steaks to a new level.**

2 TEASPOONS FOUR-PEPPERCORN BLEND, OR 1 TEASPOON BLACK PEPPERCORNS

1 TEASPOON YELLOW MUSTARD SEEDS

1 TEASPOON CUMIN SEEDS

1 TEASPOON DRIED OREGANO

1 TEASPOON DRIED THYME

1 TEASPOON SWEET PAPRIKA, PREFERABLY HUNGARIAN OR SPANISH

1 TEASPOON GARLIC POWDER

1 TEASPOON ONION POWDER

1. Heat an empty small skillet over medium heat. Have a lid handy. Add the peppercorns, mustard seeds, and cumin seeds. Cook, stirring occasionally, until the spices are aromatic and toasted (you may see a wisp of smoke), about 1 minute. If the spices jump out of the pan when heating, cover the skillet with the lid.

2. Transfer the toasted spices to an electric spice grinder or a mortar and pestle and cool. Grind the toasted spices coarsely. Add the oregano, thyme, paprika, garlic powder, and onion powder and pulse to combine well. (The spice rub can be made up to 2 months ahead, stored in an airtight container in a cool, dark place at room temperature.)

THE ULTIMATE SPICE RUB

MAKES ABOUT ⅔ CUP, ENOUGH FOR 8 POUNDS OF MEAT, POULTRY, OR SEAFOOD

With a little of this and a little of that, this **rub is so multifaceted** that you will have a hard time deciding what *not* to put it on. Skillet-toasting the spices brings out their essential oils and heightens their flavor. For an extra layer of smokiness, **use Spanish smoked paprika,** such as pimentón de La Vera.

1 TABLESPOON CUMIN SEEDS

1 TABLESPOON FENNEL SEEDS

3 TABLESPOONS SWEET PAPRIKA, PREFERABLY HUNGARIAN OR SPANISH

1 TABLESPOON DRIED THYME

1 TABLESPOON DRIED SAGE

1 TABLESPOON DRIED OREGANO

2½ TEASPOONS FRESHLY GROUND BLACK PEPPER

2 TEASPOONS ONION POWDER

2 TEASPOONS GARLIC POWDER

1 TEASPOON CAYENNE PEPPER

1. Heat an empty small skillet over medium heat. Have a lid handy. Add the cumin and fennel seeds. Cook, stirring occasionally, until the spices are aromatic and toasted (you may see a wisp of smoke), about 1 minute. If the spices jump out of the pan when heating, cover the skillet with the lid.

2. Transfer the toasted spices to an electric spice grinder or a mortar and pestle and cool. Grind the toasted spices coarsely. Add the paprika, thyme, sage, oregano, pepper, onion powder, garlic powder, and cayenne and pulse to combine well. (The rub can be made up to 2 months ahead, stored in a cool, dark place in an airtight container at room temperature.)

SPICE RUBS AND FLAVORING PASTES

- Every cook who has mastered the art of grilling has his or her favorite spice blend. With very little effort, these sassy mixtures bring bold flavor to grilled meat, poultry, and seafood.

- Spice rubs are dry mixtures of ground spices and herbs. Flavoring pastes are wet, and include moist ingredients like oil or garlic. Spice rubs can be stored in a cool, dark place in an airtight container for a couple of months. Use flavoring pastes immediately after making them.

- Spices (the edible seeds, bark, berries, buds, or roots of aromatic plants used for seasoning) contain essential oils that come to the fore when toasted. (The oils in herbs, the edible leaves of aromatic plants, are different and don't benefit from toasting.) The best way to toast spices is in a heated skillet. Have a lid handy, just in case the heated spices jump out of the skillet as they toast. Cool the spices before grinding.

- Grind spices in an electric coffee grinder reserved for the job. Be sure to use a rotary blade model, and not one with burrs. If you want to use your existing coffee grinder, remove the coffee flavor by processing ¼ cup sugar or raw rice in the grinder (and repeat with more sugar or rice to remove the spice flavor before grinding coffee!) A mortar and pestle is a low-tech option. The Japanese mortars with rough, crenellated interiors are better for grinding spices than the smooth, marble ones. If you have neither a grinder nor a mortar, crush the spices under a heavy saucepan on your work counter. The results will be quite coarse, but it works.

- To moisten the spice rub and reduce scorching, the food is sometimes brushed with a very thin layer of oil. Be sure this is a very light coating, or the oil will drip on the coals and make flare-ups.

- Whether or not you actually rub the spice coating into the food is up to you, as some spices, like paprika and cayenne, may stain and irritate your skin. If you want to rub in the spices, protect your fingers with a sheet of plastic wrap or use a rubber spatula to do the job.

- To best control the seasoning, these spice rubs do not contain salt. You should season the meat directly with salt as you prefer. Allow about 1 tablespoon of spice rub for every pound of meat; feel free to use more or less according to taste.

- If your rub calls for paprika, use smoked paprika to add an immediate smoky-spicy flavor to your cooking. Usually from the La Vera region of Spain, it is sometimes labeled "pimentón de La Vera."

TEX-MEX RUB

MAKES ABOUT ⅓ CUP, ENOUGH FOR UP TO 9 POUNDS OF MEAT

Use this on Lone Star Beef Brisket (page 90) or anytime you want **chile-infused** flavors on your **beef, pork, or chicken.** Note that chili powder, the familiar spice blend, has a base of ground mild chiles with added seasonings like oregano and cumin. Chili powder is usually used to season a pot of chili (spelled with an *i* at the end), and it is not the same as pure ground chiles (such as those made from an ancho or chipotle).

2 TEASPOONS CUMIN SEEDS

2 TABLESPOONS CHILI POWDER

2 TEASPOONS DRIED OREGANO

1 TEASPOON GARLIC POWDER

1 TEASPOON ONION POWDER

½ TEASPOON CAYENNE PEPPER

1. Heat an empty small skillet over medium heat. Have a lid handy. Add the cumin seeds. Cook, stirring occasionally, until the cumin is aromatic and toasted (you may see a wisp of smoke), about 1 minute. If the seeds jump out of the pan when heating, cover the skillet with the lid.

2. Transfer the cumin to an electric spice grinder or a mortar and pestle and cool. Grind the cumin coarsely. Add the chili powder, oregano, garlic powder, onion powder, and cayenne and pulse to combine well. (The rub can be made up to 2 months ahead, stored in a cool, dark place in an airtight container at room temperature.)

ESPRESSO-CHILE RUB

Dark roast coffee may sound like an unlikely rub, but mixed with other ingredients (including two kinds of dried chiles) into a rub, it adds deep, rich flavor to **steaks.**

2 TEASPOONS CUMIN SEEDS

2 TABLESPOONS DARK ROAST (ESPRESSO, FRENCH-, OR ITALIAN-ROAST) COFFEE BEANS

1 TABLESPOON GROUND ANCHO CHILES

½ TEASPOON GARLIC POWDER

¼ TEASPOON GROUND CHIPOTLE CHILES

1. Heat an empty small skillet over medium heat. Have a lid handy. Add the cumin seeds. Cook, stirring occasionally, until the cumin is aromatic and toasted (you may see a wisp of smoke), about 1 minute. If the seeds jump out of the pan when heating, cover the skillet with the lid.

2. Transfer the cumin to an electric spice grinder or a mortar and pestle and cool. Grind the cumin coarsely. Add the coffee beans, ground ancho chiles, garlic powder, and ground chipotle chiles and pulse to combine well. (The rub can be made up to 2 months ahead, stored in a cool, dark place in an airtight container at room temperature.)

GROUND CHILES

Not all chiles are created equal. Not only do they range enormously in their spiciness, but you will find nuances of other flavors like smoke and sugar behind the heat. No longer do you have to travel to a Latino market to find chiles, as the large spice manufacturers now carry ground versions of the most useful chiles, ancho and chipotle. Ancho has a sweet undertone, and chipotle is fiery and smoky at the same time. If you can't find them at your supermarket, they are easy to find online.

INDIAN SPICE RUB

MAKES ABOUT ¼ CUP, ENOUGH FOR 4 POUNDS OF MEAT OR POULTRY

This **fragrant mix** was developed with **lamb** in mind, but there's no reason why it couldn't grace **pork, beef, or chicken.**

1½ TEASPOONS CORIANDER SEEDS

1½ TEASPOONS CUMIN SEEDS

½ TEASPOON YELLOW MUSTARD SEEDS

½ TEASPOON WHOLE BLACK PEPPERCORNS

½ TEASPOON GROUND GINGER

¼ TEASPOON CRUSHED HOT RED PEPPER

1. Heat an empty small skillet over medium heat. Have a lid handy. Add the coriander, cumin, and mustard seeds and the peppercorns. Cook, stirring occasionally, until the spices are aromatic and toasted (you may see a wisp of smoke), about 2 minutes. If the spices jump out of the pan when heating, cover the skillet with the lid.

2. Transfer the toasted spices to an electric spice grinder or a mortar and pestle and cool. Grind the toasted spices coarsely. Add the ginger and hot pepper and pulse to mix well. (The rub can be made up to 1 month ahead, stored in an airtight container at room temperature.)

MEDITERRANEAN HERB PASTE

MAKES ABOUT ⅓ CUP, ENOUGH FOR 5 POUNDS OF MEAT OR POULTRY

This **versatile wet rub** will bring the flavors of the Mediterranean to your grilled meats and poultry. It is particularly delicious on **lamb, veal, and chicken.** If you wish, use chopped fresh herbs—just double the measurements of the rosemary and thyme, but retain the dried oregano, as fresh lacks zip.

3 TABLESPOONS EXTRA-VIRGIN OLIVE OIL

1 TABLESPOON DRIED ROSEMARY

1 TEASPOON DRIED OREGANO

1 TEASPOON DRIED THYME

2 GARLIC CLOVES, CRUSHED THROUGH A PRESS

¼ TEASPOON CRUSHED HOT RED PEPPER

Whisk the oil, rosemary, oregano, thyme, garlic, and hot pepper together in a small bowl. Use immediately.

CHERMOULA

You'll find plenty of uses for this **cilantro herb paste.** The Moroccans serve it as a sauce with **fish and poultry,** but it works equally well as a marinade, as shown in the Moroccan Chicken Kebabs with Carrot-Scallion Salad (page 164). It lasts for a couple of weeks, so you may also find yourself stirring a tablespoon or two into **salad dressings or cooked rice or couscous.**

2 GARLIC CLOVES, CRUSHED UNDER A KNIFE AND PEELED

1 CUP PACKED CILANTRO LEAVES (SEE NOTE), OR 1/2 CUP CILANTRO LEAVES AND 1/2 CUP PARSLEY LEAVES

3 TABLESPOONS FRESH LEMON JUICE

3/4 TEASPOON GROUND CORIANDER

3/4 TEASPOON GROUND CUMIN

3/4 TEASPOON SWEET PAPRIKA, PREFERABLY HUNGARIAN OR SPANISH

1 TEASPOON SALT

1 TEASPOON CRUSHED HOT RED PEPPER FLAKES

3/4 CUP EXTRA-VIRGIN OLIVE OIL

1. With the machine running, drop the garlic through the feed tube of a food processor fitted with the metal chopping blade to mince the garlic.

2. Add the cilantro, lemon juice, coriander, cumin, paprika, salt, and hot pepper. With the machine running, gradually add the oil. Transfer to a bowl. (The chermoula can be stored for up to 2 weeks, covered and refrigerated. Stir well before using.)

Note: The easiest way to remove the leaves from a bunch of cilantro or parsley is with a large sharp knife. Shear off the leaves where they meet the stems. Sort through the sheared leaves and remove any thick stems, but a few stems won't hurt. Transfer the leaves to a large bowl filled with cold water and agitate them well to dislodge any dirt. Drain well, and spin dry in a salad spinner.

WHITE WINE BRINE

MAKES ABOUT 10 CUPS, ENOUGH FOR A 6-POUND CHICKEN

Soak your **chicken** in this brine before grilling, and the flavors of **wine and herbs** will be revealed in every bite. Try it with **pork** loin or pork chops, too.

ONE 750-ML BOTTLE DRY WHITE WINE, SUCH AS PINOT GRIGIO OR SAUVIGNON BLANC

1/3 CUP PLAIN SALT

1/3 CUP FIRMLY PACKED BROWN SUGAR

1 TABLESPOON DRIED ROSEMARY

1 TABLESPOON DRIED THYME

1 TEASPOON WHOLE BLACK PEPPERCORNS

2 BAY LEAVES

7 CUPS ICE WATER

1. Bring the wine, salt, brown sugar, rosemary, thyme, peppercorns, and bay leaves to a boil in a nonreactive medium saucepan over high heat, stirring to dissolve the salt and sugar. Transfer to a nonreactive large bowl. Cool for 15 minutes, stirring often.

2. Add the ice water and stir until the ice melts and the brine is cold. Use immediately.

APPLE CIDER BRINE

MAKES ABOUT 2 GALLONS, ENOUGH FOR A 12-POUND TURKEY

Frozen apple juice concentrate brings **fruity sweetness** to this brine, which will do wonders for your **holiday turkey.** Do not brine frozen or kosher turkeys, which have already been soaked in salty solutions.

1¹/₄ CUPS PLAIN SALT

2 TABLESPOONS DRIED ROSEMARY

2 TABLESPOONS DRIED SAGE

1 TABLESPOON WHOLE BLACK PEPPERCORNS

3 BAY LEAVES

5 QUARTS ICE WATER

TWO 12-OUNCE CONTAINERS FROZEN APPLE JUICE CONCENTRATE

Bring 1 quart of water, the salt, rosemary, sage, peppercorns, and bay leaves to a boil in a medium saucepan over high heat, stirring to dissolve the salt and sugar. Transfer to a large bowl and add the ice water and apple juice concentrate. Stir until the brine is well chilled. Use immediately.

VARIATIONS

Small Batch Apple Cider Brine: This makes enough brine for 4 pork chops. It uses hard apple cider instead of apple juice concentrate. Bring one 12-ounce bottle hard apple cider, ¹/₄ cup plain salt, 1 teaspoon dried rosemary, 1 teaspoon sage, and ¹/₂ teaspoon whole black peppercorns to a boil over high heat. Pour into a bowl and stir in 2¹/₂ cups iced water.

Apple Cider and Bourbon Brine: Substitute 2 cups bourbon for an equal amount of the ice water in the Apple Cider Brine. Or add ¹/₂ cup bourbon to Small Batch Apple Cider Brine (no need to substitute for ice water).

- Many grill cooks have discovered brining to be a great method for adding moisture to some meats and poultry. It is basically an insurance policy against overcooking lean foods like pork tenderloins and chops, chicken, and turkey. Do not use it for protein foods with a fair amount of intramuscular fat marbling, such as beef, pork shoulder, or lamb.

- There are different theories about why brining works. One theory says that the heavily saturated salty solution forces itself into the meat cells. When the meat is lifted out of the brine, the flavorful solution is trapped inside of the meat.

- Before brining, look closely at the labels on the meat or poultry to be sure that no sodium products were used in processing. Many "fresh" pork products ranging from tenderloins to chops and frozen or kosher poultry have already been "enhanced" with a sodium solution. Brine one of these foods, and you will have inedible, over-salted results.

- Because of varying crystal sizes, different brands of kosher salt measure differently by volume. To avoid confusion, simply use regular plain (non-iodized) table salt for your brine.

- Use nonreactive utensils for making the brine and soak the meat in a nonreactive container. Nonreactive materials will not react with the salt (or the acids) in the brine. Stainless steel, anodized aluminum, and enameled cast iron work well for both pots and containers. It is hard to find a proper container for brining a large turkey without some searching, but you can rig up a brining setup with a large turkey roasting bag and an ice chest. Restaurant supply shops also sell large plastic containers (think in terms of gallons, not quarts) that do the job perfectly.

- Brining food for longer than recommended will not deepen the flavor—it will only toughen the meat. Allow 12 to 24 hours for turkeys, 6 to 8 hours for large (5 to 7 pounds) roasting chickens and pork loin roasts, 4 to 8 hours for average-size (up to 5 pounds) chickens, and 4 to 6 hours for pork tenderloins or pork chops. Do not reuse the brine.

BEER AND MUSTARD BRINE

Use your favorite **mellow lager beer** for this brine—ale is too bitter and stout is too dark. This brine is great with **pork.**

ONE 12-OUNCE CAN LAGER BEER, CHILLED

1/4 CUP VEGETABLE OIL

2 TABLESPOONS GRAINY DIJON MUSTARD

2 TABLESPOONS LIGHT BROWN SUGAR

2 TABLESPOONS PLAIN SALT

1 SCALLION, WHITE AND GREEN PARTS, CHOPPED

2 GARLIC CLOVES, MINCED

Whisk the beer, oil, mustard, brown sugar, salt, scallion, and garlic together in a medium bowl to dissolve the salt. Use immediately.

FLAVORED BUTTERS

Butter is pretty darned good on its own, but mixed with herbs, spices, or other seasonings, it can become one of the most useful flavorings in a grill cook's repertoire. Its lush richness can enhance many foods—melt a pat on grilled steak or chops, or toss with grilled vegetables and fruit, and they go from simple to spectacular.

The procedure to make flavored butters is constant—soften unsalted butter and mix in seasonings. The butter is kept at room temperature to allow the ingredients to mingle, but also to keep the butter at a soft consistency for easy melting over hot foods. Flavored butters can also be made ahead, refrigerated for a couple of weeks or frozen for a couple of months. Spread an 8-inch-long log of the flavored butter about 2 inches from the bottom of a 12-inch square of waxed paper. Fold the bottom of the waxed paper up to cover the butter. Pick up the waxed paper–wrapped butter by the ends of the paper. Twist the ends of the waxed paper closed in opposite directions, like a piece of taffy, to tighten the paper and compact the butter into a cylinder. The butter can now be refrigerated or frozen. Cut off pats of the firm butter as needed, but bring to room temperature before using.

You'll find recipes for Mint, Herbed Shallot, Spicy Lime, and Lime-Ginger flavored butters on pages 114, 202, 211, and 242. Here are some other easy ideas for jazzing up a stick of butter:

Herb Butter: Using a rubber spatula, mix and mash 8 tablespoons (1 stick) softened unsalted butter with 2 tablespoons minced fresh basil, tarragon, or dill in a small bowl. Season with salt and pepper to taste.

Roasted Garlic Butter: Using a rubber spatula, mix and mash 8 tablespoons (1 stick) softened unsalted butter with 2 tablespoons mashed grill-roasted garlic (page 64) in a small bowl. Season with salt and pepper to taste.

Roquefort Butter: Using a rubber spatula, mix and mash 8 tablespoons (1 stick) softened unsalted butter with 2 ounces softened Roquefort or other blue cheese in a small bowl. Season with pepper to taste.

Shallot–Red Wine Butter: Boil 1/4 cup hearty red wine, such as Cabernet-Shiraz blend, with 2 tablespoons minced shallot in a small saucepan over high heat until the liquid is reduced to 1 tablespoon, about 3 minutes. Transfer to a small bowl and cool. Add 8 tablespoons (1 stick) softened unsalted butter and mix and mash with a rubber spatula. Season with salt and pepper to taste.

PIRI-PIRI

The classic **hot table sauce of Portugal,** this spicy concoction is also served with gusto in North Africa and just about anywhere the Portuguese occupied. Like similar rustic sauces, it can be used as a marinade as well as a condiment. It gains heat as it stands, so be prepared to dilute it with a bit more olive oil, if needed, **to tone it to taste.**

3 GARLIC CLOVES, CRUSHED UNDER A KNIFE AND PEELED

4 FRESH HOT RED CHILES, SUCH AS SERRANO

1 TEASPOON SWEET PAPRIKA, PREFERABLY HUNGARIAN OR SPANISH

1 TEASPOON DRIED OREGANO

1 TEASPOON SALT

1 CUP EXTRA-VIRGIN OLIVE OIL

1/3 CUP RED WINE VINEGAR

1. With the machine running, drop the garlic through the feed tube of a food processor fitted with the metal chopping blade to mince the garlic. Add the chiles, paprika, oregano, and salt, and pulse to mince the chiles.

2. Transfer the chile mixture to a 1-pint jar or another nonreactive covered container. Add the oil and vinegar and shake well. Let stand at room temperature for least 2 hours to blend the flavors. (The piri-piri can be stored for up to 2 months, covered and refrigerated.) Shake well before using.

APPETIZERS AND SNACKS

EGGPLANT AND BASIL DIP

MAKES ABOUT 2 CUPS
Grilling Method: Indirect High

Eggplant goes through a **dramatic transformation** when grilled whole—the big purple bulb deflates to a blackened shrivel of its former self. Looks are deceiving, because the interior flesh becomes **creamy and delicious** and the beginning of an appetizing dip. Consider making a double batch, as it also is a great spread for lamb sandwiches and a fine sauce for rich-flavored fish like grilled sea bass.

TWO 1½-POUND EGGPLANTS

2 GARLIC CLOVES, CRUSHED UNDER A KNIFE AND PEELED

½ CUP (2 OUNCES) CRUMBLED RINDLESS GOAT CHEESE (CHÈVRE), PLUS MORE FOR GARNISH

2 TEASPOONS FRESH LEMON JUICE

2 TABLESPOONS EXTRA-VIRGIN OLIVE OIL, PLUS MORE FOR GARNISH

2 TABLESPOONS CHOPPED FRESH PARSLEY

SALT AND FRESHLY GROUND BLACK PEPPER TO TASTE

PITA BREAD, CUT INTO WEDGES, FOR SERVING

1. Build a charcoal fire in an outdoor grill for indirect high grilling (see page 10) and let burn until the coals are almost completely covered with white ash. You will not need a drip pan.

2. Pierce each eggplant a few times with the tines of a meat fork. Place the eggplant over the cooler area of the grill and cover. Grill without turning until the eggplant is shriveled and tender, about 40 minutes. Transfer to a plate and cool until easy to handle. Cut the eggplant open and use a spoon to scoop out the tender flesh, discarding the skin.

3. With the machine running, drop the garlic through the feed tube of food processor fitted with the metal chopping blade. Add the eggplant, goat cheese, and lemon juice and process until smooth. With the machine still running, add the oil. Add the parsley and pulse once or twice, just until combined. Season with the salt and pepper. Transfer to a bowl, cover, and refrigerate to blend the flavors, at least 1 hour. (The dip can be made up to 2 days ahead.)

4. To garnish, sprinkle the dip with goat cheese and drizzle with oil. Serve chilled or at room temperature with the pita bread.

PANCETTA-WRAPPED SHRIMP WITH ROSEMARY

MAKES 12 APPETIZERS, 3 TO 4 SERVINGS
Grilling Method: Banked

Italian food is famous for its **elegant simplicity,** and this quality is illustrated in this land-meets-sea appetizer that uses just a few well-chosen ingredients. **Use the largest shrimp** you can find, as small shrimp will be overdone by the time the pancetta crisps. Usually called U-15, meaning "under fifteen pieces to a pound," they can also be labeled "jumbo" or "colossal" shrimp.

1 TABLESPOON EXTRA-VIRGIN OLIVE OIL

1½ TEASPOONS FINELY CHOPPED FRESH ROSEMARY

1 GARLIC CLOVE, CRUSHED THROUGH A PRESS

½ TEASPOON FRESHLY GROUND BLACK PEPPER

12 (U-15, JUMBO, OR COLOSSAL) SHRIMP, PEELED AND DEVEINED, TAIL SEGMENT ATTACHED

12 SLICES PANCETTA (NOT PAPER THIN), ABOUT 4 OUNCES (SEE NOTE)

12 WOODEN TOOTHPICKS, SOAKED IN COLD WATER FOR AT LEAST 30 MINUTES, DRAINED

1. Mix the oil, rosemary, garlic, and pepper together in a medium bowl. Add the shrimp and mix to coat. Unwind the pancetta slices. Starting at the straightest end, cut off a 2- to 3-inch length of pancetta; save the curved portion for another use. Wind a pancetta slice around each shrimp and secure with a soaked toothpick. Cover and refrigerate while building the fire.

2. Build a charcoal fire in an outdoor grill for banked grilling (see page 10) and let burn until the coals are almost completely covered with white ash.

3. Lightly oil the grill grate. Place the shrimp over the hotter area of the grill and cover. Grill until the pancetta on the underside is beginning to crisp, about 3 minutes. Turn and grill until the other side is crisped, about 2 minutes. Transfer to a platter and serve hot.

Note: Pancetta is Italian bacon, and although it is made from the same cut of pork as American bacon, the meat is rolled into a cylinder and cured, not smoked. It is easily found at Italian delicatessens, and many supermarkets carry it, too. Ask the counter person to slice it about ¹⁄₁₆ inch thick, a bit thicker than the paper-thin slices for prosciutto. If you can't find it, for this recipe you can use American bacon cut into 3-inch lengths. Par-cook the American bacon in a microwave oven on High for about 30 seconds, or until the bacon is translucent and curls at the edges, then cool before using.

BARBECUED OYSTERS

MAKES 4 APPETIZER SERVINGS
Grilling Method: Indirect High

Bodega Bay, just north of San Francisco, supplies the city with some of its best oysters. The restaurants in this rural area have made a specialty of grilled oysters, dabbed with a bit of **spicy barbecue sauce** and a pat of butter to create a terrific appetizer. The shellfish are often cooked directly on the grill, but nestled in a bed of coarse salt in a cast-iron skillet, they won't tip and lose their **precious juices.** Speaking of those juices, serve the oysters with crusty bread to sop them up.

COARSE (KOSHER) SALT, FOR THE SKILLET

ABOUT ⅓ CUP ORANGE-CHIPOTLE BARBECUE SAUCE (PAGE 22), OR YOUR FAVORITE

4 TABLESPOONS UNSALTED BUTTER, CUT INTO 4 EQUAL PATS, THEN QUARTERED TO MAKE 16 SMALL CUBES

16 OYSTERS, SHUCKED BY THE FISH PURVEYOR (SEE "SHUCKING OYSTERS," PAGE 53)

CRUSTY BREAD, FOR SERVING

1. Build a charcoal fire in an outdoor grill for indirect high grilling (see page 10) and let burn until the coals are almost completely covered with white ash. You will not need a drip pan.

2. Fill a 12-inch-diameter cast-iron skillet with a ½-inch-thick layer of coarse salt. Place 1 teaspoon barbecue sauce and a cube of butter in each oyster shell. Nestle the oysters shell side down in the salt. If necessary, balance some of the oysters on top of the bottom layer.

3. Place the skillet on the empty side of the grill and cover. Grill just until the edges of the oyster flesh begins to curl, about 8 minutes.

4. Using tongs, transfer 4 oysters to each of 4 plates, taking care not to tip them and spill the juices. Serve hot, with the bread.

SHUCKING OYSTERS

Your fish purveyor may carry oysters, but it is becoming increasingly difficult to have them opened at the store. It is a good idea to know how to shuck them yourself.

You can buy oyster knives, with sturdy blades and upturned tips, at kitchen shops. However, you may already have an even more effective shucking tool in your kitchen drawer—a punch-style can opener, sometimes called a "church key" opener. Its sharp pointed tip is perfect for prying open the clutched oyster shells.

Place an oyster, concave side down, on the work surface. Use a pot holder or thick towel to hold the oyster and protect your holding hand. At the pointed end of the oyster, locate the seam where the two shell halves meet. With the sharp pointed tip of the can opener facing up, wedge the tip at the seam between the two halves—this takes some elbow grease. Once the tip has been inserted, push down on the can opener (like a lever) to pry the shells apart. Remove the can opener and run a small knife between the edges of the shells to separate them completely. Pull the shells apart. The oyster will remain attached to the flatter shell half. Slide the knife under the oyster to cut and release it from the shell. Place the oyster in the curved shell. To keep the oysters from tipping over, place crumpled aluminum foil in a baking dish, and balance the oysters in the creased foil folds. Refrigerate and use the oysters within a few hours of shucking.

FORK-AND-KNIFE STUFFED MUSHROOMS

MAKES 4 SERVINGS
Grilling Method: Banked

Serve these **hearty sausage-stuffed** portobello mushrooms as a plated first course. Their dark gills can give off a lot of inky juices that will make the stuffing soggy, so the trick is to scrape out most of the gills before filling the caps. A side salad of **green arugula** helps brighten up the colors on the plate.

SALAD

1 TABLESPOON RED WINE VINEGAR

SALT AND FRESHLY GROUND BLACK PEPPER TO TASTE

1/4 CUP EXTRA-VIRGIN OLIVE OIL

4 CUPS LOOSELY PACKED ARUGULA, TOUGH STEMS REMOVED

STUFFING

1 TABLESPOON EXTRA-VIRGIN OLIVE OIL, PLUS MORE FOR BRUSHING THE MUSHROOMS AND DRIZZLING OVER THE STUFFING

8 OUNCES PORK OR TURKEY ITALIAN SAUSAGE, CASINGS REMOVED

2 TABLESPOONS CHOPPED SHALLOTS

2 GARLIC CLOVES, MINCED

1 CUP FRESH BREAD CRUMBS

1 TEASPOON CHOPPED FRESH ROSEMARY OR 1/2 TEASPOON DRIED ROSEMARY

1 LARGE EGG, BEATEN

1/4 TEASPOON SALT

1/8 TEASPOON FRESHLY GROUND BLACK PEPPER

FOUR 4-INCH-DIAMETER PORTOBELLO MUSHROOMS, STEMS TRIMMED

1. To make the salad, first make vinaigrette by whisking the vinegar with a pinch of salt and a grind or two of pepper in a small bowl. Gradually whisk in the oil. Adjust the seasoning, and set the vinaigrette aside.

2. To make the stuffing, heat the oil in a medium skillet over medium heat. Add the sausage and cook, breaking up the meat with a spoon, until the sausage loses its pink color, about 6 minutes. Add the shallots and garlic and cook until they soften, about 2 minutes more. Transfer to a bowl. Stir in the bread crumbs and rosemary, and then the egg, salt, and pepper.

3. Using a dessert spoon, scrape out most of the black gills from the undersides of the mushroom caps (don't be fussy about this, and leave a few strips of gills to supply some juices), being sure not to break the caps. Brush the caps all over with olive oil. Fill the caps with the stuffing, and drizzle a little oil over the tops. Set aside while building the fire.

4. Build a charcoal fire in an outdoor grill for banked grilling (see page 10) and let burn until the coals are almost completely covered with white ash.

5. Lightly oil the grill grate. Place the mushrooms over the hotter area of the grill and cover. Grill until the undersides of the mushrooms are seared, about 2 minutes. Move to the cooler area of the grill, cover, and grill until the mushrooms are tender and the stuffing is lightly browned, about 4 minutes. Transfer the mushrooms to a plate.

6. Toss the arugula and vinaigrette in a large bowl and divide among 4 dinner plates. Top each salad with a mushroom and serve immediately.

QUESADILLAS WITH GRILLED CHILES

MAKES 8 SERVINGS
Grilling Method: Direct High

Grilling not only enhances the flavor of chiles, but it also blackens their skin to make it easier to remove. Dark green, heart-shaped **poblano chiles,** which are usually stuffed for such dishes as chiles rellenos, are put to good use here in quesadillas. Sometimes called anchos on the West Coast, these are **just hot enough** to tell the difference between them and bell peppers. (Just don't confuse them with dried ancho chiles, which are, in fact, processed from fresh poblanos/anchos.) If you wish, substitute red bell peppers.

2 FRESH POBLANO (ANCHO) CHILES

1 CUP (4 OUNCES) SHREDDED SHARP
　CHEDDAR CHEESE

1 CUP (4 OUNCES) SHREDDED MONTEREY JACK

EIGHT 7-INCH-DIAMETER FLOUR TORTILLAS

STORE-BOUGHT SALSA, FOR SERVING

1. Build a charcoal fire in an outdoor grill for direct high grilling (see page 8) and let burn until the coals are almost completely covered with white ash.

2. Place the chiles on the grill and cover. Grill, turning occasionally, until the skin is blistered and charred on all sides, 10 to 15 minutes; take care to grill just until the skins are blackened and do not grill a hole through the flesh. Transfer to a plate and cover the grill to keep the coals from burning down too quickly.

3. Cool the chiles until easy to handle. Remove and discard the charred skin. Cut the chiles open, discard the seeds, and cut lengthwise into strips.

4. Combine the cheddar and Monterey Jack cheeses. Place 4 tortillas on a work surface and sprinkle each with $\frac{1}{2}$ cup of the mixed cheese. Top each with one-fourth of the chile strips. Place the remaining 4 tortillas on top of the cheese-topped ones to make 4 sandwiched quesadillas.

5. Carefully place the quesadillas on the grill. Cover and grill until undersides are toasted, about 2 minutes. Carefully turn and grill to toast the other sides, about 2 minutes more. Transfer to a cutting board and cut each into 6 to 8 wedges. Arrange the wedges on a platter. Spoon a dab of salsa on each wedge and serve hot.

EASY NACHOS

A **cast-iron skillet** used to be an essential kitchen utensil. With the advent of easier-to-care-for metals, it is now considered a specialty item—unless you are a griller. This heatproof beauty retains heat like nobody's business, and keeps hot appetizers warm while serving. (There are also earthenware dishes that do the trick, although the skillet is more versatile in the long run.) Put a skillet of these **simple nachos** in front of your guests, and count the minutes before the chips are outta here.

8 OUNCES (A LITTLE MORE THAN HALF A 14-OUNCE BAG) TORTILLA CHIPS

ONE 16-OUNCE CAN REFRIED BEANS

½ CUP PICKLED JALAPEÑO STRIPS

2 CUPS (8 OUNCES) SHREDDED MONTEREY JACK OR SHARP CHEDDAR CHEESE, OR A COMBINATION

STORE-BOUGHT SALSA, FOR SERVING

1. Build a charcoal fire in an outdoor grill for indirect high grilling (see page 10) and let burn until the coals are almost completely covered with white ash. You will not need a drip pan.

2. Put half of the tortilla chips in a 9- to 10-inch-diameter cast-iron skillet or heatproof earthenware dish. Spoon half of the beans over the chips, then sprinkle with half of the jalapeño strips and half of the cheese. Repeat with the remaining chips, beans, jalapeños, and cheese.

3. Place on the empty side of the grill and cover. Grill until the cheese melts, about 6 minutes. Scatter the salsa over the top and serve hot.

MORE IDEAS FOR NACHOS

Rev up the flavor of your nachos with one or more of the following:

- 2 cups chopped barbecued chicken or beef
- 2 cups carnitas (slow-simmered pork cubes, available at Mexican delicatessens)
- 1 cup rinsed and drained canned black beans
- 2 small zucchini, diced, sautéed in olive oil until lightly browned
- 3 ounces hard chorizo, diced and sautéed until browned

SMOKY TOMATO SOUP

MAKES 4 SERVINGS
Grilling Method: Direct High

In this updated version of the **lunchtime classic,** tomatoes and poblano chiles are grilled to remove their skins, pumping up their flavor in the process. Their smokiness is transferred to the soup pot, making this **one of the tastiest tomato soups around.** For the most intense flavor, make the soup when plum tomatoes are at their seasonal peak. A bit of cornstarch stabilizes the heavy cream, which could curdle in contact with the acidic tomatoes.

2 POUNDS RIPE PLUM (ROMA) TOMATOES

1 HANDFUL MESQUITE WOOD CHIPS, SOAKED IN COLD WATER FOR AT LEAST 30 MINUTES, DRAINED

1 FRESH POBLANO (ANCHO) CHILE OR RED BELL PEPPER

1 TABLESPOON EXTRA-VIRGIN OLIVE OIL

1 MEDIUM ONION, CHOPPED

1 MEDIUM CELERY RIB, CHOPPED

2 GARLIC CLOVES, MINCED

2 CUPS CHICKEN STOCK, PREFERABLY HOMEMADE, OR USE CANNED REDUCED-SODIUM BROTH

1 TABLESPOON TOMATO PASTE (OPTIONAL)

1 TEASPOON CORNSTARCH

¼ CUP HEAVY CREAM, PLUS MORE FOR GARNISH

SALT AND FRESHLY GROUND BLACK PEPPER TO TASTE

1. Build a charcoal fire in an outdoor grill for direct grilling (see page 8) and let burn until the coals are almost completely covered with white ash.

2. Cut each tomato in half lengthwise. Working over a sieve placed over a medium bowl, using your finger, poke the seeds out of the tomatoes. Press the seeds in the sieve with a rubber spatula to extract the juice, discard the seeds, and reserve the juice.

3. Toss the drained wood chips on the coals. Place the chile on the grill and cover. Grill, turning occasionally, until the skin is blistered and charred on all sides, 10 to 15 minutes. Take care to grill just until the skins are blackened and do not grill a hole through the chile flesh. Transfer the chile to a plate.

4. Add the tomatoes to the grill, skin sides down. Grill, uncovered (to check their progress better) until the tomato skins are blistered, about 3 minutes. Turn and grill until the cut sides are seared with grill marks, about 1 minute. Transfer to the plate with the chile. Cool until the chile and tomatoes are easy to handle. Remove and discard the charred skins. Cut the chile open and discard the seeds. Coarsely chop the chile and tomatoes.

5. Heat the oil in a medium saucepan over medium heat. Add the onion and celery and cook, stirring often, until the onion is softened, about 5 minutes. Add the garlic and cook until it is fragrant, about 1 minute. Add the tomatoes and chile and cover. Cook until the tomatoes give off juices, about 5 minutes. Add the chicken stock and bring to a boil. If the soup needs a stronger tomato flavor, whisk in the tomato paste. Reduce the heat to medium-low and simmer, stirring occasionally, until the tomatoes are very tender, about 15 minutes. Sprinkle the cornstarch over 1 tablespoon of cold water in a small bowl and stir to dissolve; add the heavy cream. Stir the cream mixture into the soup and return to a simmer. Season with salt and pepper and serve hot, garnishing each serving with a drizzle of cream.

SWEET, STICKY, AND SPICY CHICKEN WINGS

MAKES 34 WINGETTES, ABOUT 6 SERVINGS
Grilling Method: Indirect High

Serve these **mouthwatering wings** to close friends who don't mind licking their fingers in public. The wings sport at least **four layers of flavor**—the chicken itself, a zesty spice rub, a fruity-savory glaze, and smokiness from the grill.

3½ POUNDS (ABOUT 17 PIECES) CHICKEN WINGS

1½ TEASPOONS KOSHER SALT

1 TEASPOON GROUND CINNAMON

1 TEASPOON GROUND CUMIN

¼ TEASPOON GARLIC POWDER

¼ TEASPOON CAYENNE PEPPER

ONE 9-OUNCE JAR MANGO CHUTNEY, SUCH AS MAJOR GREY

2 TABLESPOONS POMEGRANATE MOLASSES OR BALSAMIC VINEGAR

1. Chop the wings between the joints into 3 pieces. Discard the wing tips or save for another use. In a small bowl, mix the salt, cinnamon, cumin, garlic powder, and cayenne together. Season the chicken wings with the spice mixture. Cover and refrigerate while building the fire.

2. Build a charcoal fire in an outdoor grill for indirect high grilling (see page 10) and let burn until the coals are almost completely covered with white ash.

3. Meanwhile, pulse the chutney and pomegranate molasses in a food processor until the chunky bits of mango are minced. Transfer to a bowl and set aside.

4. Lightly oil the grill grate. Place the wings on the cooler area of the grill and cover. Grill for 15 minutes. Turn the wings and cook until they are browned and show no sign of pink when pierced at the thickest part near a bone, about 20 minutes longer. During the last few minutes, brush the tops of the wings with half of the chutney mixture.

5. Turn the wings, moving them to the hotter area, directly over the coals. Brush with the remaining chutney mixture. Cook, turning occasionally, until the wings are glazed, about 2 minutes. (Although most of the fat will have cooked away by this point, the wings are likely to flare up, so adjust the final glazing time as needed.) Transfer to a platter and serve hot.

ROASTED GARLIC AÏOLI WITH SUMMER VEGETABLES

MAKES ABOUT 2 CUPS AÏOLI
Grilling Method: Banked

In the south of France, aïoli (eye-OH-lee) is such a **popular dip for fresh vegetables** that some villages have festivals around the garlicky mayonnaise, not unlike our fish fries and chicken feeds. Sure, you can mix **roasted garlic** into some bottled mayonnaise, but it is very easy to make aïoli from scratch, and you'll have more authentic flavor in the bargain. You may not want to fire up briquets just to roast a couple of heads of garlic, so think ahead and toss the garlic on the grill when you're cooking another meal, as the roasted heads will keep for a few days. Note that the homemade mayonnaise contains a raw egg—use about 1⅔ cup bottled mayonnaise if you prefer.

ROASTED GARLIC

2 FIRM, PLUMP GARLIC HEADS

1 TEASPOON EXTRA-VIRGIN OLIVE OIL

SALT AND FRESHLY GROUND BLACK PEPPER TO TASTE

MAYONNAISE

1 LARGE EGG

1 TEASPOON DIJON MUSTARD

1 TEASPOON FRESH LEMON JUICE

¾ CUP OLIVE OIL (NOT EXTRA-VIRGIN)

¾ CUP VEGETABLE OIL

SALT AND FRESHLY GROUND BLACK PEPPER TO TASTE

ASSORTED FRESH VEGETABLES (SUCH AS RAW CARROT, CELERY, CUCUMBER, ZUCCHINI, AND FENNEL STICKS; STRIPS OF RED BELL PEPPER; HALVED CHERRY TOMATOES; AND BOILED BABY POTATOES), FOR SERVING

1. Build a charcoal fire in an outdoor grill for banked grilling (see page 10) and let burn until the coals are almost completely covered with white ash.

2. To roast the garlic, cut about ½ inch from the top of each garlic head to make "lids." Drizzle ½ teaspoon oil over the cut surface of each and season with salt and pepper. Replace the lids to return the garlic heads to their original shapes. Wrap each head in aluminum foil.

3. Place over the cooler part of the grill and cover. Grill until the garlic is very tender and the flesh is golden-beige, about 40 minutes. Unwrap and cool. Squeeze the tender garlic flesh from the hulls into a small bowl. Mash the flesh with a fork and set aside.

4. To make the mayonnaise, place the uncracked egg in a small bowl of hot tap water and let stand for 5 minutes to warm it slightly. Crack the egg into a food processor or blender. Add the mustard and lemon juice. Mix the olive and vegetable oils in a small bowl. With the machine running, slowly pour the oils through the feed tube—it should take about 1 minute to add the oil. Season with salt and pepper. Add the garlic and pulse to combine. Transfer to a serving bowl.

HONEY-ANCHO PECANS

MAKES 1 POUND
Grilling Method: Indirect High

These nibbles are virtually **impossible to resist**—put them out for your guests to snack on while you tend the grill, and you are likely to come back to an empty bowl. They make great homemade holiday gifts, too. Dried ancho chiles have a sweet note, and you can now find them, ground into a powder, in the spice rack at most supermarkets. Chili powder will work, too. Some people will find these nuts perfectly seasoned, and others may want to add a bit **more kick with cayenne,** so the final choice is up to you.

4 CUPS (1 POUND) PECAN HALVES

¼ CUP HONEY

¼ CUP LIGHT CORN SYRUP

1 HANDFUL MESQUITE WOOD CHIPS, SOAKED IN COLD WATER FOR AT LEAST 30 MINUTES, DRAINED

3 TABLESPOONS SUGAR

2 TEASPOONS GROUND DRIED ANCHO CHILES OR CHILI POWDER

2 TEASPOONS GROUND CUMIN

2 TEASPOONS SWEET PAPRIKA, PREFERABLY HUNGARIAN OR SPANISH

1 TEASPOON SALT

⅛ TEASPOON CAYENNE PEPPER (OPTIONAL)

1. Build a charcoal fire in an outdoor grill for indirect high grilling (see page 10) and let burn until the coals are almost completely covered with white ash. You will not need a drip pan.

2. Mix the pecans, honey, and corn syrup together in a 13 × 9-inch disposable aluminum pan. Toss the drained chips on the coals. Place the pan over the cooler area of the grill and cover. Grill, stirring occasionally, until the liquid has almost completely evaporated, about 20 minutes.

3. Meanwhile, mix the sugar, ground chiles, cumin, paprika, salt, and cayenne, if using, in a large bowl and set aside.

4. Scrape the syrup-coated pecans into the bowl and mix well, separating any nuts that cling to each other. Turn out onto a rimmed baking sheet and cool completely. Store the pecans in an airtight container. (The pecans can be made up to 1 week ahead.)

BEEF

THE BEST BURGERS

To grill **great burgers,** start with the right grind of beef. Chuck is a bit too fatty (and causes flare-ups that would make Mt. Vesuvius proud), and sirloin too lean, but round has just the right fat content for **juiciness and flavor.** Although even round beef is likely to drip fat on the coals, have no fear, as the pocket grilling method provides a clear, coal-free space to move them.

1½ POUNDS GROUND ROUND BEEF (85% LEAN)

1 TEASPOON SALT

½ TEASPOON FRESHLY GROUND BLACK PEPPER

4 HAMBURGER BUNS

MAYONNAISE, KETCHUP, MUSTARD, LETTUCE, SLICED TOMATOES, ONIONS, AND PICKLES, FOR SERVING

1. Mix the ground round, salt, and pepper in a medium bowl. Form into four 4-inch patties. Handle the meat lightly and do not pack it, or the burgers will be coarse-textured and dry. Place on a waxed paper–lined plate, cover, and let stand at room temperature while building the fire.

2. Build a charcoal fire in an outdoor grill for pocket grilling (see page 11) and let burn until the coals are almost completely covered with white ash.

3. Lightly oil the grill grate. Place the burgers on the grill and cover. Cook, turning often, moving the burgers that drip fat and flare up to the cleared pockets in the coals, until the burgers are well browned and feel somewhat firm when pressed in the center, about 6 minutes for medium–rare, or longer if desired. If using an instant-read thermometer, insert it horizontally through the side of the burger to reach the center—it should read 125°F. During the last 2 minutes, place the buns on the grill to toast lightly and warm through.

4. Place a burger in each bun and serve hot, with the fixings passed on the side.

VARIATION

Cheese Burgers: During the last 2 minutes of grilling, top each burger with about ¼ cup (1 ounce) shredded cheddar or Monterey Jack cheese, or 1 slice American cheese.

BIG, BOLD BACON BURGERS

MAKES 4 SERVINGS
Grilling Method: Pocket

For super-size appetites, a huge half-pound burger might be in order. **Lots of spices** and a thick slather of barbecue sauce make these burgers appropriate for burger lovers who like oversize flavors, too. With the **barbecue sauce,** you can skip the traditional condiments, but you still might like tomato, onion, and lettuce.

8 SLICES BACON

2 POUNDS GROUND ROUND BEEF (85% LEAN)

2 TEASPOONS SALT

¾ TEASPOON FRESHLY GROUND BLACK PEPPER

4 TEASPOONS STEAKHOUSE RUB (PAGE 32)

1 CUP ALL-AMERICAN BARBECUE SAUCE (PAGE 18), OR YOUR FAVORITE STORE-BOUGHT SAUCE

4 HAMBURGER BUNS

LETTUCE, SLICED TOMATOES, AND SLICED ONIONS, FOR SERVING

1. Cook the bacon in a medium-size skillet over medium heat until crisp and browned, about 8 minutes. Transfer the bacon to paper towels to drain and cool. Cut each bacon strip in half.

2. Mix the ground round, salt, and pepper in a medium bowl. Form into four thick 4-inch patties. Handle the meat lightly and do not pack it, or the burgers will be coarse-textured and dry. Sprinkle the rub on both sides of the patties. Place on a waxed paper-lined plate, cover, and let stand at room temperature while building the fire.

3. Build a charcoal fire in an outdoor grill for pocket grilling (see page 11) and let burn until the coals are almost completely covered with white ash.

4. Lightly oil the grill grate. Place the burgers on the grill and cover. Cook, turning often, moving the burgers that drip fat and flare up to the clear pockets in the coals, until the burgers are well browned and feel somewhat firm when pressed in the center, about 6 minutes for medium-rare, or longer if desired. If using an instant-read thermometer, insert it horizontally through the side of the burger to reach the center—it should read 125°F. During the last 2 minutes, brush the burgers with the sauce so they are coated on both sides, and place the buns on the grill to toast lightly and warm through.

5. Place a burger in each bun with 4 half-slices of bacon, and serve hot, with the lettuce, tomatoes, and onions passed on the side.

NEW YORK STRIP STEAKS WITH STEAKHOUSE RUB

MAKES 4 SERVINGS
Grilling Method: Banked

Depending on where you live, this **invaluable addition** to the steak menu can be called strip steak, Kansas City steak, New York steak, shell steak, or top loin steak. If you are having trouble picturing it, it is the large portion of a T-bone steak, which kind of has the profile of New York State. While this steak is perfectly fine without any embellishments, the addition of this rub will remind you of your best meals at your **favorite steakhouse.**

STEAKHOUSE RUB

2 TEASPOONS FOUR-PEPPERCORN BLEND, OR ½ TEASPOON BLACK PEPPERCORNS

1 TEASPOON YELLOW MUSTARD SEEDS

1 TEASPOON CUMIN SEEDS

1 TEASPOON DRIED OREGANO

1 TEASPOON DRIED THYME

1 TEASPOON SWEET PAPRIKA, PREFERABLY HUNGARIAN OR SPANISH

1 TEASPOON GARLIC POWDER

1 TEASPOON ONION POWDER

FOUR 14-OUNCE TOP LOIN (ALSO CALLED NEW YORK, KANSAS CITY, OR STRIP) STEAKS, CUT ABOUT ¾ INCH THICK

SALT TO TASTE

1. To make the rub, heat a small skillet over medium heat and have a lid handy. Add the peppercorns, mustard seeds, and cumin seeds. Cook, stirring occasionally, until the spices are aromatic and toasted (you may see a wisp of smoke), about 1 minute. If the spices jump out of the pan when heating, cover the skillet with the lid. Transfer the toasted spices to an electric spice grinder or a mortar and pestle and let cool for a minute or two. Grind the toasted spices coarsely. Add the oregano, thyme, paprika, garlic powder, and onion powder and pulse to combine well.

2. Season the steaks with salt, then sprinkle with the rub. Cover and let stand while building the fire.

3. Build a charcoal fire in an outdoor grill for banked grilling (see page 10) and let burn until the coals are almost completely covered with white ash.

4. Lightly oil the grill grate. Place the steaks over the hotter area of the grill. Cover and grill until the undersides are seared with grill marks, about 2 minutes. Turn the steaks and sear the other sides, about 2 minutes more. Move to the cooler area of the grill and cover. Grill, turning once, until an instant-read thermometer inserted at the side of the steak into the center reads 125°F, 3 to 4 minutes for medium-rare, or longer if desired. Transfer each steak to a dinner plate and serve.

ESPRESSO-RUBBED FLANK STEAK WITH TOASTED CORN AND PEPPERS

MAKES 4 SERVINGS
Grilling Method: Direct High

Flank steak is at its best when grilled, as long as you **don't overcook it.** Well-done flank steak equals tough flank steak, so if you like your steak cooked more than medium-rare, consider another cut.

ONE 1½-POUND FLANK STEAK

SALT TO TASTE

4 TEASPOONS ESPRESSO-CHILE RUB (PAGE 37)

TOASTED CORN AND PEPPERS

1 TABLESPOON OLIVE OIL

1 SMALL RED BELL PEPPER, SEEDS AND RIBS REMOVED, CUT INTO ¼-INCH DICE

3 CUPS (ABOUT 4 LARGE EARS) FRESH CORN KERNELS, CUT FROM THE COB

1 TABLESPOON UNSALTED BUTTER

SALT AND FRESHLY GROUND BLACK PEPPER TO TASTE

1. Season the steak with salt. Sprinkle with the rub. Cover and let stand at room temperature while building the fire.

2. Build a charcoal fire in an outdoor grill for direct high grilling (see page 8) and let burn until the coals are almost completely covered with white ash.

3. Meanwhile, make the corn and peppers. Heat the oil in a heavy medium-size skillet, preferably cast iron, over medium heat. Add the bell pepper and cook, stirring often, until tender, about 4 minutes. Transfer the peppers to a plate. Add the corn to the skillet and increase the heat to medium-high. Cook, stirring occasionally, until lightly browned around the edges, about 5 minutes. Return the peppers to the skillet, add the butter, and cook until the peppers are reheated, about 1 minute. Season with salt and pepper. Reheat before serving.

4. Lightly oil the grill grate. Place the steak on the grill and cover. Grill, turning occasionally, until the steak is well browned and feels somewhat firm when pressed in the thickest part, about 8 minutes for rare meat. It is more reliable to use your sense of touch and sight to judge the doneness, as it is difficult to insert a thermometer into a thin flank steak.

5. Transfer the steak to a carving board with a well and let stand for 5 minutes. Reheat the corn, if necessary. Holding the knife at a 45-degree diagonal, cut the meat into thin slices across the grain of the steak. Serve hot, with the carving juices poured over the steak, and with the corn and peppers.

HANGER STEAKS WITH CHIMICHURRI SAUCE

MAKES 4 TO 6 SERVINGS
Grilling Method: Direct High

The hanger steak may be a **newfound darling** of restaurant chefs, but it has been around forever at Jewish butchers, where it is known as Romanian tenderloin (and it does indeed look like actual beef tenderloin). The steak requires an easy but unusual way of preparing for the grill so you'll get two long steaks of different weights and thicknesses. For four moderate servings, cut up both sections and offer both large and small slices. Or, depending on appetites, you could serve half of each steak to make two large portions. The chimichurri sauce, a verdant green **Argentine parsley sauce** (think of it as South American pesto), is a piquant condiment for the steak.

CHIMICHURRI SAUCE

1 GARLIC CLOVE, CRUSHED UNDER A KNIFE AND PEELED

¾ CUP PACKED FRESH PARSLEY, PREFERABLY ITALIAN FLAT LEAF

2 SCALLIONS, WHITE AND GREEN PARTS, COARSELY CHOPPED

2 TABLESPOONS RED WINE VINEGAR

1 TEASPOON DRIED OREGANO

¼ TEASPOON CRUSHED HOT RED PEPPER

¼ TEASPOON SALT

½ CUP EXTRA-VIRGIN OLIVE OIL

TWO 1¾-POUND HANGER STEAKS

SALT AND FRESHLY GROUND BLACK PEPPER TO TASTE

1. To make the chimichurri sauce, with the machine running, drop the garlic through the feed tube of a food processor or blender to mince it. Add the parsley, scallions, vinegar, oregano, hot pepper, and salt and process to chop the parsley. With the machine running, gradually add the oil. Transfer to a serving bowl and let stand at room temperature for 1 hour to blend the flavors. (The sauce can be made up to 1 day ahead, covered and refrigerated. Return to room temperature before serving.)

2. Place 1 steak on the work surface. Locate the long sinew that runs down the length of the steak. Pull the two sections of the steak apart at this sinew. Trim away the gristle from each section. You will have two long steaks, one thicker than the other. Repeat with the second steak. Season with salt and pepper. Cover and let stand at room temperature while building the fire.

3. Build a charcoal fire in an outdoor grill for direct high grilling (see page 8) and let burn until the coals are almost completely covered with white ash.

4. Lightly oil the grill grate. To give the larger steaks a head start, place them on the grill and cover. Grill, turning once, for 3 minutes. Add the smaller steaks to the grill and cover. Grill, turning all steaks occasionally, until an instant-read thermometer inserted in the center of the large steak reads 125°F for medium-rare, about 7 minutes longer. The smaller steak may be too thin to get an accurate reading with a thermometer, so you should use your sense of touch and sight to judge its doneness—it should be nicely browned and feel somewhat firm when pressed.

5. Transfer the steaks to a carving board with a well and let stand for 5 minutes. Cut across the grain of the meat into ½-inch-thick slices. Serve the steak hot on dinner plates, with the chimichurri sauce passed on the side.

HANGER STEAK

This tough but very flavorful cut gets its name from the way it hangs from the flank area on the steer. Like its neighbors on the cattle musculature, flank and skirt, it should be cooked no more than medium-rare, or it will dry out. Do not confuse this cut with skirt steak, regardless of what you might read in some sources.

KOREAN RIB EYE STEAK WITH KIM CHEE SLAW

MAKES 4 SERVINGS
Grilling Method: Banked

Korea is famous for its grilled steaks. Butterflied short ribs are most popular, possessing a chewy texture that the Koreans love. Rib eye steaks are next in line in popularity, and appropriate for Westerners, who prefer their steaks less tough.

KIM CHEE SLAW

ONE 4-INCH LENGTH FRESH GINGER, PEELED AND SHREDDED (ON THE LARGE HOLES OF A BOX GRATER)

2 TABLESPOONS RICE VINEGAR

2 TABLESPOONS SUGAR

1 TEASPOON HOT OR SWEET PAPRIKA

1/2 TEASPOON CRUSHED HOT RED PEPPER, OR MORE TO TASTE

1/3 CUP VEGETABLE OIL

2 TABLESPOONS DARK ASIAN SESAME OIL

6 CUPS (ABOUT 1 1/4 POUNDS) CORED AND SHREDDED NAPA CABBAGE

4 SCALLIONS, WHITE AND GREEN PARTS, CHOPPED

2 TEASPOONS SESAME SEEDS

SALT TO TASTE

KOREAN MARINADE (PAGE 31)

FOUR 1-POUND RIB EYE STEAKS

1. To make the slaw, squeeze the ginger in your fist over a medium bowl to extract the juice. You should have 2 tablespoons juice. Add the vinegar, sugar, paprika, and red pepper. Whisk in the vegetable and sesame oils. Mix in the cabbage, scallions, and sesame seeds, then season with salt. Cover and refrigerate for at least 1 hour, or up to 8 hours.

2. Divide the marinade and steaks between two 1-gallon resealable plastic bags. Close the bags and let stand at room temperature while building the fire. (The steaks can be refrigerated for up to 8 hours, but remove from the refrigerator 1 hour before grilling.)

3. Build a charcoal fire in an outdoor grill for banked grilling (see page 10) and let burn until the coals are almost completely covered with white ash.

4. Lightly oil the grill grate. Remove the steaks from the marinade, but do not pat dry. Place the steaks over the hotter area of the grill and cover. Cook until the undersides are seared with grill marks, about 2 minutes. Turn and sear the other side, about 2 minutes more. Move to the cooler area of the grill and cook, turning once, until the steaks feel somewhat firm when pressed in the center, about 3 minutes for medium-rare, or longer if desired. It is more reliable to use your sense of touch and sight to judge the doneness, as it is difficult to insert a thermometer into a steak. If you want to try, insert the thermometer horizontally through the side of the steak to reach the center—it should read 125°F for medium-rare.

5. Transfer each steak to a dinner plate, add equal amounts of the slaw, and serve immediately.

TUSCAN T-BONE STEAKS WITH GARLIC SPINACH

MAKES 4 SERVINGS
Grilling Method: Banked

European beef can't hold a candle to American cattle, but there is an Italian breed, the Chianina, that is justly famous. Grass-fed in Tuscany, its meat is often cut into T-bone steaks, simply grilled, and served with **garlicky spinach.** American steaks take well to this unfussy treatment, too.

GARLIC SPINACH

THREE 10-OUNCE BAGS LEAF SPINACH, TOUGH STEMS REMOVED

2 TABLESPOONS EXTRA-VIRGIN OLIVE OIL

2 GARLIC CLOVES, FINELY CHOPPED

SALT AND FRESHLY GROUND BLACK PEPPER TO TASTE

FOUR 1¼-POUND T-BONE STEAKS, CUT ABOUT 1 INCH THICK

1½ TABLESPOONS EXTRA-VIRGIN OLIVE OIL, PLUS MORE FOR DRIZZLING

SALT AND FRESHLY GROUND BLACK PEPPER TO TASTE

LEMON WEDGES

1. To make the spinach, rinse the leaves in cold water. Drain, but do not spin dry. Heat the oil in a large saucepan over medium heat. Add the garlic and stir until fragrant, about 1 minute. In batches, add the spinach to the skillet and stir, letting each batch wilt before adding another. Cover and cook just until the spinach is tender, about 3 minutes. Season with salt and pepper. (The spinach can be cooked up to 2 hours ahead, covered and kept at room temperature. Reheat gently before serving.)

2. Brush both sides of each steak with the olive oil and season with salt and pepper. Let stand at room temperature while building the fire.

3. Build a charcoal fire in an outdoor grill for banked grilling (see page 10) and let burn until the coals are almost completely covered with white ash.

4. Lightly oil the grill grate. Place the steaks over the hotter area of the grill and cover. Grill until the undersides are seared with grill marks, about 2 minutes. Turn and sear the other sides, about 2 minutes more. Move to the cooler area of the grill and cover. Grill, turning once, until the steaks feel somewhat firm when pressed in the center, about 4 minutes for medium-rare, or longer if desired. It is more reliable to use your sense of touch and sight to judge the doneness, as it is difficult to insert a thermometer into a steak. If you want to try, insert the thermometer horizontally through the side of each steak to reach the center—it should read 125°F for medium-rare.

5. Divide the spinach among 4 dinner plates and top with the steak. Drizzle the steak and spinach with oil. Serve hot, with the lemon wedges.

FILETS MIGNONS WITH ROQUEFORT BUTTER AND CLASSIC POTATO GRATIN

GRILLING CLASSIC

MAKES 4 SERVINGS
Grilling Method: Banked

Many diners equate the quality of a steak with its tenderness. For those folks, filet mignon reigns supreme. Here is a version, direct from a **French bistro,** that can't be more classic, with **Roquefort butter** topping the beautifully charred steak. If you're not in the mood for Roquefort, try the Shallot–Red Wine Butter on page 45.

CLASSIC POTATO GRATIN

SOFTENED BUTTER, FOR THE BAKING DISH

1½ POUNDS BAKING POTATOES, SUCH AS RUSSET OR BURBANK, PEELED

½ TEASPOON SALT

½ TEASPOON FRESHLY GROUND BLACK PEPPER

2 CUPS HEAVY CREAM, HEATED, OR MORE AS NEEDED

FOUR 7-OUNCE FILETS MIGNONS

SALT AND FRESHLY GROUND BLACK PEPPER TO TASTE

ROQUEFORT BUTTER (PAGE 45)

1. To make the gratin, preheat the oven to 375°F. Generously butter an 11½ × 8-inch glass baking dish. Slice the potatoes thinly (a slicing tool, such as a mandoline or a food processor with the slicing blade, comes in handy here). Layer the potatoes in the dish, seasoning with the salt and pepper as you go. Pour in the hot cream, adding more if needed to barely cover the potatoes. Bake until the potatoes are tender and the top is browned, about 40 minutes.

2. Season the filets mignons with salt and pepper. Let stand at room temperature while building the fire.

3. Build a charcoal fire in an outdoor grill for banked grilling (see page 10) and let burn until the coals are almost completely covered with white ash.

4. Lightly oil the grill grates. Place the steaks over the hotter area of the grill and cover. Cook until the undersides are seared with grill marks, about 2 minutes. Turn and sear the other sides, about 2 minutes more. Move to the cooler area of the grill and cook, turning once, until an instant-read thermometer inserted through the side of the steak to the center reads 125°F, about 6 minutes for medium-rare, or longer if desired.

5. Transfer each steak to a dinner plate and top with a dollop of the butter. Add a portion of the gratin to each, and serve immediately.

SPICE-RUBBED LONDON BROIL WITH GRILLED MUSHROOMS

MAKES 6 SERVINGS
Grilling Method: Banked

For price alone, London broil is a favorite cut, especially for **weeknight family meals.** A quickly made spice rub delivers lots of flavor directly to the surface of the meat. To be sure that the brown sugar in the rub does not burn, the steak should be cooked over the lower heat of the banked coals. **Skewer mushrooms** to grill alongside. The large "gourmet" mushrooms are best, but you can use whatever size you prefer and adjust the grilling time as needed.

3 TABLESPOONS PACKED LIGHT BROWN SUGAR

1½ TEASPOONS WHOLE BLACK PEPPERCORNS

1 TABLESPOON YELLOW MUSTARD SEEDS

1 TABLESPOON WHOLE CORIANDER SEEDS

4 GARLIC CLOVES, CRUSHED UNDER A KNIFE AND PEELED

1¾ POUNDS BEEF TOP ROUND STEAK, CUT 1½ INCHES THICK

16 LARGE BUTTON MUSHROOMS (SOMETIMES CALLED "GOURMET" MUSHROOMS)

OLIVE OIL, FOR BRUSHING

SALT AND FRESHLY GROUND BLACK PEPPER TO TASTE

1. Process the brown sugar, peppercorns, mustard and coriander seeds, and garlic in a blender until the seeds are crushed. Brush the beef and mushrooms with olive oil. Season the steak with salt. Spread the spice rub on both sides of the steak. Thread the mushrooms on each of 4 metal skewers, and season the mushrooms with salt and pepper. Let stand at room temperature while building the fire.

2. Build a charcoal fire in an outdoor grill for banked grilling (see page 10) and let burn until the coals are almost completely covered with white ash.

3. Lightly oil the grill grate. Place the steak over the cooler area of the grill and cover. Grill for 6 minutes. Turn the steak. Place the mushrooms over the hotter area of the grill and cover. Cook, turning the mushrooms occasionally, until the steak feels somewhat firm when pressed in the center and the mushrooms are browned and tender, about 6 minutes for medium-rare steak, or longer if desired. If the mushrooms are done before the steak, slide them off their skewers into a bowl and cover with aluminum foil to keep warm.

4. Transfer the steak to a carving board and let stand 5 minutes. Cut across the grain into thin, diagonal slices. Serve immediately, with the mushrooms

TEX-MEX BEEF KEBABS

MAKES 4 SERVINGS
Grilling Method: Banked

If you're looking for a tender steak, top round would not be the first choice. However, cut into cubes, it makes **great, flavor-packed kebabs.** (This is because its long fibers are cut into smaller pieces, which make for easier eating.) Rubbed with Southwestern seasonings, skewered with corn and sweet red peppers, and finished with a chipotle sauce, these kebabs are for chile lovers and their friends. Use **long metal skewers** for these, as wooden skewers are not sturdy enough to pierce the corn cob. If you have trouble piercing the cob, use a meat mallet to pound in the skewer—it's easier than it sounds.

1¾ POUNDS TOP ROUND, CUT INTO SIXTEEN 2-INCH CUBES

4 TEASPOONS VEGETABLE OIL

SALT TO TASTE

2 TABLESPOONS TEX-MEX RUB (PAGE 36)

4 EARS CORN, HUSKS AND SILKS REMOVED, EACH TRIMMED AND CUT CROSSWISE INTO 4 EQUAL PIECES

1 LARGE RED BELL PEPPER, SEEDS AND RIBS REMOVED, CUT INTO 16 PIECES ABOUT 1¼ INCHES SQUARE

FRESHLY GROUND BLACK PEPPER TO TASTE

½ CUP ORANGE-CHIPOTLE BARBECUE SAUCE (PAGE 22)

1. Have ready 4 long metal skewers. Toss the beef in a medium-size bowl with 2 teaspoons of the oil. Season with salt, sprinkle with the spice rub, and toss again. Toss the corn and red pepper squares in another bowl with the remaining 2 teaspoons of oil, season with salt and pepper, and toss again. Thread 4 beef cubes, 4 corn pieces, and 4 red pepper squares onto each skewer, alternating the ingredients as you wish. Cover and let stand at room temperature while building the fire. (The kebabs can be prepared up to 1 day ahead, covered, and refrigerated. Remove from the refrigerator 30 minutes before grilling.)

2. Build a charcoal fire in an outdoor grill for banked grilling (see page 10) and let burn until the coals are almost completely covered with white ash.

3. Lightly oil the grill grate. Place the kebabs over the hotter area of the grill and cover. Grill, turning once, until lightly browned on all sides, about 3 minutes. Move to the cooler area of the grill. Brush the beef cubes with half of the sauce. Cover and grill for 2 minutes. Turn the kebabs, brush with the remaining sauce, cover, and grill until the meat feels somewhat firm when pressed, about 2 minutes longer for medium-rare, or longer if desired. Transfer to a large platter.

4. Let the kebabs stand for 3 to 5 minutes. Slide the beef and vegetables off each skewer onto 4 dinner plates. Serve hot.

PRIME RIB WITH PEPPER-MUSTARD RUB

MAKES 4 TO 6 SERVINGS
Grilling Method: Indirect High

Few dishes set a **festive mood** for a special holiday dinner like prime rib. To fully enjoy its beefy richness, treat it simply and let the meat **speak for itself.** In this recipe, the enhancing flavors are kept to a minimum of mustard, salt, and peppers.

ONE 5-POUND (2-RIB) BEEF RIB ROAST

SALT TO TASTE

2 TABLESPOONS DIJON MUSTARD

2 TABLESPOONS FOUR-PEPPERCORN BLEND (SEE NOTE), OR 1 TEASPOON BLACK PEPPERCORNS

1 TABLESPOON YELLOW MUSTARD SEEDS

MEAT AU JUS, MADE WITH BEEF BONES (PAGE 109), OR USE HIGH-QUALITY PREPARED BEEF STOCK

1. Using a thin sharp knife, trim away most of the fat cap from the roast. Season the roast all over with salt. Spread the top of the roast (from where the fat was trimmed) with the mustard. Mix the four-peppercorn blend and mustard seeds on a sheet of waxed paper. Turn the roast upside down and roll it in the mixed spices, evenly coating the mustard-topped area. Cover and let stand while building the fire.

2. Build a charcoal fire in an outdoor grill for indirect high grilling (see page 10) and let burn until the coals are almost completely covered with white ash.

3. Lightly oil the grill grate. Pour 1 cup of water into a drip pan. Place the roast, pepper side up, over the drip pan and cover. Adjust the grill vents so they are half-open. Grill for about 1 hour. The temperature will start out high, then level out. Add 12 briquets to the coals to maintain the heat and cover again. Grill for about 40 minutes or until an instant-read thermometer inserted in the center of the roast reads 125°F for medium-rare meat.

4. Transfer the roast to a platter and let stand for 10 to 20 minutes. Carve the roast and serve hot, au jus.

Note: You'll find this mix of black, white, pink, and green peppercorns in specialty markets, at many supermarkets, and online. It is sometimes called rainbow peppercorn blend, and it may be made with five types of peppercorn.

LONE STAR BEEF BRISKET

In Texas, **barbecue means brisket.** Sure, you can find ribs and links and other smoked meats, but brisket is king. There are few pleasures greater than biting into a tender slice of rubbed, smoked, and sauced brisket. Start by getting **a whole brisket** with all of its surface fat intact from a cooperative butcher, as the trimmed briskets you find at a supermarket can't stand up to 6 hours of smoking.

ONE 8- TO 10-POUND WHOLE UNTRIMMED BEEF BRISKET

SALT TO TASTE

1/3 CUP TEX-MEX RUB (PAGE 36)

4 OR 5 HANDFULS MESQUITE WOOD CHIPS, SOAKED IN WATER FOR AT LEAST 30 MINUTES

TWO 12-OUNCE BOTTLES LAGER BEER

ALL-AMERICAN BARBECUE SAUCE (PAGE 18)

8 TO 12 SOFT SANDWICH ROLLS

1. Trim some of the fat from the surface of the brisket, but leave a layer about ¼ inch thick. Season the brisket with salt. Sprinkle with the rub. Cover and let stand at room temperature for 1 hour.

2. Build a charcoal fire in an outdoor grill for indirect low grilling (see page 9) and let burn until the coals are almost completely covered with white ash.

3. Lightly oil the grill grate. Add 2 cups of water to a drip pan. Toss a handful of chips on the coals. Place the brisket over the drip pan. Cover and smoke the brisket until it is fork tender and a meat thermometer inserted in the thickest part reads 185°F, 5 to 6 hours. After about an hour, and every hour or so after that, moisten the brisket with some of the beer, and add 10 briquettes and a handful of chips to the coals to maintain a temperature of 300° to 325°F. Be flexible with the grilling time. The finished brisket will be very dark brown, almost black.

4. Transfer the brisket to a carving board and let stand for 20 minutes. Using a thin-bladed knife, slice the brisket across the grain. Do not be alarmed about a dark pink ring at the exterior—the smoke has colored the meat at this area. Using a large, heavy knife, coarsely chop the lean and fatty parts of the brisket, and mix them together. Place the chopped brisket in a bowl.

5. Serve the chopped brisket with the sauce and rolls so guests can make their own sandwiches.

BARBECUE USA

The definition of *barbecue*—slowly cooked meat infused with smoke—changes from state to state, and in some cases, from town to town. Traditionally, the determining factor was the availability of local meat and wood. Texas barbecue evolved from beef and mesquite; Carolina "cue" from pork shoulder and hickory; Memphis likes hickory-smoked pork ribs with spice rub but not sauce; Georgia residents serve up both shoulder and ribs, often smoked with fruit wood and glazed; Santa Maria is known for barbecued beef, cooked over oak, always served with beans California-style. While it is not technically referred to as barbecue, the Northwest has its salmon cooked over alder, maple, or cedar. And the Northwest owns the clambake (if you consider seaweed a kind of wood). No matter where you eat it and what it is called, this unique American culinary institution is usually delicious.

MARINATED BEEF TENDERLOIN

Surely one of the **classiest meals** you can serve from the grill, beef tenderloin is always a crowd pleaser, and it feeds a crowd, too. Directions are included for trimming down the vacuum-packaged whole tenderloins that you are likely to buy at a price club, as learning how to do this minor butchering will save substantial cash. If you wish, pay the premium for a trimmed, tied roast.

ONE 6½-POUND UNTRIMMED WHOLE BEEF TENDERLOIN

HERBED RED WINE MARINADE (PAGE 24), OR TERIYAKI MARINADE (PAGE 30)

1. Open the package and drain the beef. Rinse well under cold running water, but do not be concerned about any odor, which will dissipate in a minute or two. Using a sharp, thin-bladed knife, trim away and discard the fat, including the large lump of fat at the wide end. Pull and cut away the long, thin "chain" muscle that runs the length of the tenderloin. (If you wish, trim away the fat from the chain and reserve the meat for another use.) Following the natural muscle separation, cut away the large clod of meat at the wide end and reserve for another use. (This clod and the chain make great kebabs.) At one end of the meat, make an incision under the sliver sinews covering the meat. Slip the knife under the sinew, and pull and trim it away. Work lengthwise down the tenderloin until it is completely free of sinew and fat. Fold the thin ends of the tenderloin underneath so the roast is the same thickness. With twine, tie the roast throughout its length at 2-inch intervals, being sure to secure the thin ends down.

2. Place the tenderloin in a 1-gallon resealable plastic bag. Add the marinade and close the bag. Let stand at room temperature for 1 hour or refrigerate for up to 8 hours. If refrigerated, remove from the refrigerator 1 hour before grilling.

3. Build a charcoal fire in an outdoor grill for indirect high grilling (see page 10) and let burn until the coals are almost completely covered with white ash.

4. Lightly oil the grill grate. Pour 2 cups of water into a drip pan. Drain the tenderloin and pat dry with paper towels. Place the tenderloin over the coals and cover. Grill, turning occasionally, until seared on all sides, about 10 minutes. Move the tenderloin over the pan.

5. Continue roasting until an instant-read thermometer inserted in the center of the roast reads 130°F for medium-rare meat, about 20 minutes, or longer if desired. Check the meat's temperature often to avoid overcooking.

6. Let the tenderloin stand for 5 minutes before removing the twine. Carve crosswise into ½-inch-thick slices and serve.

SANTA MARIA BARBECUED BEEF WITH SOUPY BEANS

MAKES 8 SERVINGS
Grilling Method: Banked

If you find yourself on **California's Central Coast,** it is worth any detour to sample the famous barbecued beef of Santa Maria, charcoal grilled with oak from double-thick top loin steaks. (In the last few years, tri-tip roast, a cut hard to find outside of California, has been supplanting top loin, but the original cut is no slouch.) If there is a secret to these meaty slabs, it is to **keep it simple.** The rub is nothing more than salt, pepper, and garlic powder, and there is no sauce. Accompaniments rarely vary from mildly spiced beans (Santa Marians use the local piquinto, but you can make do with pink beans), green salad, crusty bread, and, it goes without saying, plenty of red wine.

SOUPY BEANS

1 TABLESPOON OLIVE OIL

4 BACON STRIPS, COARSELY CHOPPED

1 MEDIUM ONION, CHOPPED

2 GARLIC CLOVES, CHOPPED

FOUR 19-OUNCE CANS PINK BEANS, DRAINED AND RINSED

ONE 15-OUNCE CAN MILD ENCHILADA SAUCE

2 TABLESPOONS TOMATO PASTE

TWO 2½-POUND TOP SIRLOIN STEAKS, CUT 3 INCHES THICK (SEE NOTE)

1½ TEASPOONS SALT, PREFERABLY COARSE (KOSHER)

1 TEASPOON FRESHLY GROUND PEPPER

½ TEASPOON GARLIC POWDER

STORE-BOUGHT SALSA, FOR SERVING

1. To make the beans, heat the oil in a large heavy-bottomed saucepan over medium heat. Add the bacon and cook, stirring often, until the bacon is crisp around the edges but not entirely cooked, about 4 minutes. Add the onion and cook, stirring, until softened, about 5 minutes. Stir in the garlic and cook until fragrant, about 1 minute. Add the beans, enchilada sauce, and tomato paste and stir to dissolve the paste. Bring to a simmer, reduce the heat to medium-low, and simmer until the beans are heated through, about 10 minutes. (The beans can be made up to 2 hours ahead, kept at room temperature. Or cook, cover, and refrigerate for up to 2 days. To reheat, add ¼ cup water and cook over medium-low heat, until the beans are heated through, about 10 minutes.)

2. Trim the excess surface fat from the steaks. Mix the salt, pepper, and garlic powder in a small bowl. Sprinkle the salt mixture all over the steaks. Cover and let stand at room temperature until the steaks lose their chill, about 1 hour.

3. Meanwhile, build a charcoal fire in an outdoor grill for banked grilling (see page 10) and let burn until the coals are almost completely covered with white ash.

4. Lightly oil the grill grate. Place the steaks over the hottest area of the grill and cover. Grill the steaks, turning them occasionally, until they are deeply browned on all sides, about 10 minutes. The dripping fat from the steaks may cause some flare-ups, but the closed lid should keep them under control. Move the steaks to the cooler area of the grill and cover. Grill, turning occasionally, until an instant-read thermometer inserted in the center of the steaks reads 125°F for medium-rare, about 20 minutes, or longer if desired.

5. Transfer the steaks to a carving board with a well and let stand for 5 minutes. Using a thin carving knife, slice the steaks thinly. Serve hot, with the beans, salsa, and the carving juices.

Note: You can order these thick steaks from your butcher, but the easiest and most economical way is to cut them from a whole loin purchased at a price club. A whole top loin is about 9 pounds. Remove the entire roast from its wrapping, rinse under cold water, and pat dry. Cut the two large steaks with a large knife. If you wish, cut the remaining steak into individual 1-inch-thick steaks, wrap, and freeze for another meal.

VIETNAMESE BEEF SALAD WITH EYE OF ROUND

MAKES 6 TO 8 SERVINGS
Grilling Method: Banked

Here's a refreshing salad that will be welcome as the **centerpiece of a cooling meal** for a hot summer's day or night. A colorful heap of Asian vegetables is topped with thin slices of marinated and grilled eye of round. Get to know this reasonably priced cut, which gives lots of servings of grilled beef roast with very little waste. Icy glasses of beer would be a great thirst-quencher with this mildly spiced dish.

BEEF AND MARINADE

½ CUP VIETNAMESE OR THAI FISH SAUCE

ONE 2-INCH LENGTH FRESH GINGER, PEELED AND SHREDDED ON THE LARGE HOLES OF A BOX GRATER

2 TABLESPOONS LIGHT BROWN SUGAR

2 TABLESPOONS DARK ASIAN SESAME OIL

2 GARLIC CLOVES, CHOPPED

½ TEASPOON CRUSHED HOT RED PEPPER FLAKES

ONE 2-POUND EYE OF ROUND BEEF ROAST, TRIMMED AND TIED

SALAD

2 TABLESPOONS UNSEASONED RICE VINEGAR

1 TABLESPOON VIETNAMESE OR THAI FISH SAUCE

1 TABLESPOON LIGHT BROWN SUGAR

½ CUP VEGETABLE OIL

1 TABLESPOON DARK ASIAN SESAME OIL

6 CUPS (ABOUT 1¼ POUNDS) CORED AND SHREDDED NAPA CABBAGE

3 SCALLIONS, WHITE AND GREEN PARTS, FINELY CHOPPED

1 LARGE CARROT, SHREDDED

¼ CUP CHOPPED FRESH MINT

1 SMALL HOT CHILE PEPPER, SUCH AS SERRANO, SEEDED AND RIBBED, FINELY CHOPPED

SALT AND FRESHLY GROUND BLACK PEPPER TO TASTE

1. To make the marinade, whisk the fish sauce, ginger, brown sugar, sesame oil, garlic, and red pepper flakes in a small bowl. Pour into a resealable plastic bag. Add the beef roast, close, and refrigerate for at least 2 and up to 8 hours. Remove from the refrigerator 1 hour before grilling.

2. To make the salad, whisk the vinegar, fish sauce, and brown sugar in a large bowl. Gradually whisk in the vegetable and sesame oils. Add the cabbage, scallions, carrot, mint, and chile pepper, and mix well. Season lightly with salt and pepper. (The fish sauce is salty, and the chile may provide enough heat.) Cover and refrigerate for at least 1 hour before serving. (The salad can be made up to 8 hours ahead. It is best served the day it is made.)

3. Build a charcoal fire in an outdoor grill for banked grilling (see page 10) and let burn until the coals are almost completely covered with white ash.

4. Lightly oil the grill grate. Remove the beef from the marinade, but do not pat dry. Place the beef over the hotter area of the grill and cover. Grill, turning occasionally, until browned on all sides, about 6 minutes. Move to the cooler area of the grill and cover. Grill, turning occasionally, until an instant-read thermometer inserted in the center of the beef reads 125°F, about 20 minutes. Eye of round is best cooked to no more than medium-rare.

5. Transfer the beef to a carving board and let stand 10 minutes. (Or cool the beef to room temperature.) Transfer the salad to a large rimmed platter or shallow serving bowl. Using a thin, sharp knife, remove the twine and cut the beef crosswise into thin slices. Fan the slices over the salad and serve.

FISH SAUCE

One of the key flavors of Southeast Asian cooking, fish sauce is made from fermented fish or cephalopods (one very popular brand, made from squid, sports the sea animal on its label as a way to identify its flavor source). Salty and pungent, this seasoning ingredient can be found at Asian grocers and many supermarkets. The Vietnamese *(nuoc cham)* and Thai *(nam pla)* versions are very similar, but pass over the Indonesian variety *(pastis),* which is blander. If you can't find it, substitute soy sauce, which isn't the same at all, even though it will supply an Asian touch to the dish.

"DINOSAUR" BEEF RIBS

So large they are sometimes jokingly called dinosaur ribs, beef ribs are every bit as good as pork ribs on the grill. To be sure to melt away the tough stuff, give them a **long, slow smoky grill,** and use a rib rack to hold as many ribs as possible. The choice of rub and sauce is yours, but you can't go wrong with the ones recommended here.

6 POUNDS BEEF RIBS (ALSO CALLED BEEF BARBECUE RIBS), CUT INTO MANAGEABLE SLABS

SALT AND FRESHLY GROUND BLACK PEPPER TO TASTE

½ CUP THE ULTIMATE SPICE RUB (PAGE 34)

3 OR 4 HANDFULS MESQUITE WOOD CHIPS, SOAKED IN WATER FOR 30 MINUTES

ONE 12-OUNCE CAN LAGER BEER

2 CUPS ALL-AMERICAN BARBECUE SAUCE (PAGE 18)

1. Season the ribs with salt and pepper. Sprinkle with the rub. Cover and let stand at room temperature while building the fire.

2. Build a charcoal fire in an outdoor grill for indirect low grilling (see page 9) and let burn until the coals are almost completely covered with white ash.

3. Lightly oil the grill grate. Sprinkle a handful of chips on the coals. Add 2 cups water to a drip pan. Place a metal rib rack (a V-shaped roasting rack works fine) over the drip pan. Arrange the ribs on the rack, and cover. Grill until the ribs are fork-tender, about 2 hours. After about 45 minutes or so, toss another handful of chips on the coals, add 6 briquets to the coals to maintain a temperature of about 325°F, and baste with the beer to moisten the spice rub. Repeat basting and adding chips every 45 minutes. Transfer the ribs to a platter. (The ribs can be prepared to this point up to 8 hours ahead, cooled, covered, and refrigerated.)

4. Remove the rib rack from the grill. Remove the grill grate from the grill and add about 3 pounds of charcoal briquets to the coals. Let the fresh briquets burn until they are almost completely covered with white ash. Spread the coals in an even layer and let burn until they are medium-hot—you should be able to hold your hand over the coals for about 3 seconds. If the coals are too hot, the heat will encourage flare-ups. Replace the grill grate.

5. Return the ribs to the grill. Brush with half of the sauce, turn the ribs, and brush with the remaining sauce. Cover and grill until the undersides are glazed, about 2 minutes. Turn and glaze the other sides, about 2 minutes longer. Transfer to a cutting board. Let stand for 5 minutes, cut into individual ribs, and serve hot.

VEAL LOIN CHOP WITH PROSCIUTTO, SAGE, AND CHEESE

MAKES 4 SERVINGS
Grilling Method: Banked

Here's another **very simple dish** that produces excellent results. You'll be using the very best ingredients, which accounts for a lot. The high/moderate mixed heat of banked grilling cooks the veal at a rate that helps **retain its moisture.**

TOMATO-SAGE SAUCE

1 TABLESPOON UNSALTED BUTTER

1 TABLESPOON CHOPPED SHALLOT

1 GARLIC CLOVE, FINELY CHOPPED

ONE 28-OUNCE CAN WHOLE TOMATOES IN
    JUICE, DRAINED AND CHOPPED

1 TEASPOON CHOPPED FRESH SAGE

PINCH OF CRUSHED HOT RED PEPPER

FOUR 8-OUNCE VEAL LOIN CHOPS

SALT AND FRESHLY GROUND BLACK PEPPER TO TASTE

2 SLICES PROSCIUTTO, EACH CUT IN HALF CROSSWISE

4 OUNCES FRESH MOZZARELLA, THINLY SLICED

1 TABLESPOON CHOPPED FRESH SAGE

1. To make the tomato-sage sauce, melt the butter in a small saucepan over medium heat. Add the shallot and garlic and cook, stirring, until softened, about 2 minutes. Add the tomatoes, sage, and hot pepper and bring to a boil over high heat. Return the heat to medium and cook briskly until the liquid has evaporated, about 5 minutes. (The sauce can be made up to 2 hours ahead, stored at room temperature. Reheat before serving.)

2. Season the veal with salt and pepper. Cut a deep pocket through the meaty side of each chop. Stuff each chop with a half-piece of prosciutto, folding the prosciutto to fit. Cover and let stand at room temperature while building the fire.

3. Build a charcoal fire in an outdoor grill for banked grilling (see page 10) and let burn until the coals are almost completely covered with white ash.

4. Lightly oil the grill grate. Place the veal chops over the hotter area of the grill and cover. Grill until the undersides are seared with grill marks, about 2 minutes. Turn and sear the other sides, about 2 minutes more. Transfer to the cooler area of the grill and cover. Grill until the meat feels firm and springs back when pressed in the center, about 8 minutes. During the last minute, top each chop with an equal amount of sliced mozzarella.

5. Spoon equal amounts of the tomato-sage sauce on each of 4 dinner plates and top with a veal chop. Sprinkle with sage and serve immediately.

VEAL RIB CHOPS WITH ASPARAGUS VINAIGRETTE

MAKES 4 SERVINGS
Grilling Method: Banked

Mild-tasting veal chops take well to a **wine-based marinade,** which supplies another layer of flavor and adds extra moisture as well. Asparagus vinaigrette is a fine backdrop for the browned chops. You might be tempted to grill the asparagus for the salad, but sometimes too many grilled dishes on the plate can be too much of a good thing.

FOUR 10-OUNCE VEAL RIB CHOPS

HERBED WHITE WINE MARINADE (PAGE 26)

ASPARAGUS VINAIGRETTE

1½ POUNDS ASPARAGUS, WOODY ENDS TRIMMED AND DISCARDED, CUT ON THE DIAGONAL INTO 1-INCH LENGTHS

GRATED ZEST OF 1 LEMON

1½ TABLESPOONS FRESH LEMON JUICE

2 TEASPOONS FINELY CHOPPED SHALLOT

½ TEASPOON DIJON MUSTARD

SALT AND FRESHLY GROUND BLACK PEPPER TO TASTE

⅓ CUP PLUS 1 TABLESPOON EXTRA-VIRGIN OLIVE OIL

1. Place the veal in a 1-gallon resealable plastic bag and add the marinade. Close the bag and let stand at room temperature for 1 hour. (Or refrigerate for up to 8 hours and remove from the refrigerator 1 hour before grilling.)

2. To make the asparagus vinaigrette, bring a large pot of lightly salted water to a boil over high heat. Add the asparagus and cook until barely tender, about 4 minutes. Drain and rinse well under cold water. Pat the asparagus dry with paper towels.

3. Whisk together the lemon zest and juice, shallots, mustard, and salt and pepper in a medium bowl. Gradually whisk in the oil. Add the asparagus and toss well. (The asparagus can be made up to 2 hours ahead, covered, and stored at room temperature.)

4. Build a charcoal fire in an outdoor grill for banked grilling (see page 10) and let burn until the coals are almost completely covered with white ash.

5. Lightly oil the grill grate. Place the veal chops over the hotter area of the grill and cover. Grill until the undersides are seared with grill marks, about 2 minutes. Turn and sear the other sides, about 2 minutes more. Transfer to the cooler area of the grill and cover. Grill until the meat feels firm and springs back when pressed in the center, about 12 minutes.

6. Spoon equal amounts of the asparagus vinaigrette on each of 4 dinner plates and top with a veal chop. Serve immediately.

LAMB

MARINATED BUTTERFLIED LEG OF LAMB

MAKES 6 TO 8 SERVINGS
Grilling Method: Banked

In many backyards, the serving of a **sizzling leg of lamb,** hot off the grill, calls for opening up a fine bottle of Pinot Noir. This version has all of the classic elements—a lusty, herb-scented marinade, a crusty exterior, and juicy meat with a variety of doneness levels from medium-well to rare. (A leg of lamb, even butterflied, is not evenly thick, and it is impossible to cook the meat to a regulated temperature throughout.) Hope that you have leftovers for making into sandwiches.

ONE 4½-POUND BONELESS LEG OF LAMB

HERBED RED WINE MARINADE (PAGE 24)

1. Using a sharp, thin knife, trim off the excess fat from the surface of the lamb, including any nodules in the meat. Also, trim away any sinew. To butterfly the lamb, place it fat-trimmed side down on a work surface. Cut a deep incision in the thickest part of the meat, being sure not to cut all the way through, and open this flat. Repeat in two or three other thick areas of the meat—the idea is to spread the lamb out and make it as even as possible.

2. Place the lamb in a 1-gallon resealable plastic bag and add the marinade. Close the bag and let stand at room temperature while building the fire. (Or refrigerate the marinating lamb for up to 8 hours. The lamb can also be marinated in a nonreactive ceramic, glass, or stainless-steel bowl.)

3. Build a charcoal fire in an outdoor grill for banked grilling (see page 10) and let burn until the coals are almost completely covered with white ash.

4. Lightly oil the grill grate. Remove the lamb from the marinade. If you wish, to help the lamb keep its shape and make it easier to turn on the grill, insert 2 or 3 long metal skewers crosswise through the lamb. Place over the hotter area of the grill and cover. Grill until the underside is browned, about 4 minutes. Turn and grill, covered, until the other side is browned, about 4 minutes more. Move to the cooler area of the grill and cover. Grill until an instant-read thermometer inserted in the thickest part of the lamb reads 125°F for mostly medium-rare lamb (the thinner parts will have cooked more quickly and will be medium to medium-well), about 12 minutes.

5. Transfer the lamb to a carving board with a well and let stand 5 minutes. Remove the skewers, if using. Using a sharp thin knife, carve the lamb into thin slices across the grain. Place the sliced lamb on a warmed platter and pour the carving juices on top. Serve hot.

WARMED PLATTERS

Carved lamb tends to cool quickly, so it is helpful to serve it from a warmed platter. Place a heatproof platter in an oven preheated to its lowest setting for about 5 minutes. If you aren't sure if the platter is heatproof, run a thin stream of hot tap water over the platter for a few minutes to warm it, then dry well.

THREE-ROAST HERB-CRUSTED LEG OF LAMB

MAKES 6 TO 8 SERVINGS
Grilling Method: Banked

If you like your lamb medium-rare, then butterflied leg of lamb is iffy because you will get plenty of medium meat along with the rarer sections. This method separates the lamb into **three individual roasts,** so you can control the internal temperatures better. The pre-grill butchering also removes the majority of the sinew and fat that can inhibit full enjoyment of your lamb. You will have to juggle the three different cooking times, but the **tender, juicy results** are worth it.

ONE 4¾-POUND BONELESS LEG OF LAMB

SALT TO TASTE

MEDITERRANEAN HERB PASTE (PAGE 39)

1. Using a sharp, thin knife, trim off the excess fat from the surface of the lamb, including any nodules in the meat. Place the meat, fat-trimmed side down, in front of you on the work surface. You should see be able to discern three muscle formations that can be separated into individual masses—a large one on one side, a medium one on the other side, and a smaller, thinner mass between them. Following the natural demarcations in the muscle structure, cut the lamb into these 3 roasts. Take your knife and trim away any sinew or connective tissue; each finished roast should be clean red meat. Using kitchen string, tie each roast crosswise and lengthwise into compact cylinders, 1 large, 1 medium, and 1 small.

2. Season the lamb roasts with salt. Rub the herb paste all over the roasts. Cover and let stand while building the fire. (The roasts can be prepared up to 1 day ahead, covered and refrigerated. Remove from the refrigerator 30 minutes before grilling.)

3. Build a charcoal fire in an outdoor grill for banked grilling (see page 10) and let burn until the coals are almost completely covered with white ash.

4. Place the roasts over the hotter area of the grill and cover. Cook, turning occasionally, until browned on all sides, about 6 minutes. Move to the cooler part of the grill and cover. Grill, turning the roasts occasionally, until an instant-read thermometer inserted in the center of each roast reads 125°F for medium-rare. This will take about 6 more minutes for the small roast, 12 more minutes for the medium roast, and 18 more minutes for the largest roast. When each roast is done, transfer to a platter and tent with aluminum foil to keep warm. If desired, grill the lamb longer for more well done meat. Let the final roast stand for 5 minutes before carving.

5. Transfer the roasts to a carving board with a well. Remove the string and thinly slice each roast crosswise. Place the sliced meat on a warmed platter (see "Warmed Platters," page 107) and pour the carving juices on top. Serve hot, giving each guest a portion of each roast.

MEAT JUS

Although grilled lamb or beef can be perfection without a lot of bells and whistles, there are special occasions when a bit of over-the-top attitude is called for, and a spoonful of rich, meaty sauce is appropriate to make the dish *au jus*.

2 POUNDS BEEF BONES OR LAMB NECK, SAWED BY THE BUTCHER INTO LARGE CHUNKS

1 SMALL ONION, CHOPPED

1 SMALL CARROT, CHOPPED

1 GARLIC CLOVE, CRUSHED UNDER A KNIFE AND PEELED

1 TEASPOON TOMATO PASTE

¼ TEASPOON DRIED THYME

3 SPRIGS FRESH PARSLEY

½ TEASPOON WHOLE BLACK PEPPERCORNS

1. Position an oven rack 6 inches from the source of heat and preheat the broiler. Place the bones on a broiler rack. Broil, turning the bones occasionally, until browned on all sides, about 10 minutes. Pour 1 tablespoon of the rendered fat into a medium saucepan; discard the remaining fat. Transfer the bones to a plate.

2. Add the onion and carrot to the saucepan and cook over medium heat, stirring occasionally, until the onion is golden, about 8 minutes. Add the bones. Add the garlic and tomato paste, and add enough cold water to cover the bones by 1 inch, about 1½ quarts. Bring to a boil over high heat, skimming off the foam. Add the thyme, parsley, and peppercorns. Reduce the heat to very low and simmer until the stock is full-flavored, at least 2 and up to 5 hours. Do not salt the stock. Strain the stock in a colander set over a bowl. Let stand 5 minutes, then skim off any clear fat that rises to the surface. (The stock can be made up to 3 days ahead, cooled, covered, and refrigerated. Lift off the solidified fat from the surface. If you wish, freeze the stock in a covered container for up to 3 months. Defrost before using.)

3. Pour the skimmed stock into a clean medium saucepan and bring to boil over high heat. Cook until the stock is reduced to about ½ cup, about 30 minutes. Take care that the sauce does not scorch toward the end of the cooking time. Serve hot. (The sauce can be made up to 3 days ahead, cooled, covered, and refrigerated. Reheat before serving.)

LAMB KEBABS WITH INDIAN SPICES AND CUCUMBER-MINT RAITA

MAKES 4 SERVINGS
Grilling Method: Direct High

Redolent of **toasted spices,** the aroma alone of this Indian-inspired dish will have everyone at the table happy before they've even had a bite. The ingredient list may be substantial here, but the procedure is very straightforward. **A cooling raita** is the perfect accompaniment, along with some simple steamed basmati rice.

CUCUMBER-MINT RAITA

2 MEDIUM CUCUMBERS, PEELED, CUT IN HALF LENGTHWISE, SEEDS SCOOPED OUT AND DISCARDED, CUCUMBERS CUT CROSSWISE INTO ¼-INCH-THICK HALF-MOONS

1 TEASPOON SALT, PLUS MORE TO TASTE

¾ CUP PLAIN YOGURT

1 TABLESPOON CHOPPED FRESH MINT OR CILANTRO

FRESHLY GROUND BLACK PEPPER TO TASTE

1½ POUNDS BONELESS LEG OF LAMB, TRIMMED AND CUT INTO SIXTEEN 1½-INCH CUBES

4 TEASPOONS VEGETABLE OIL

SALT TO TASTE

INDIAN SPICE RUB (PAGE 38)

1 LARGE RED BELL PEPPER, SEEDS AND RIBS REMOVED, CUT INTO 16 PIECES ABOUT 1½ INCHES SQUARE

2 MEDIUM ZUCCHINI, TRIMMED AND EACH CUT INTO 8 PIECES ABOUT 1 INCH LONG

FRESHLY GROUND BLACK PEPPER TO TASTE

1. To make the raita, toss the cucumbers with 1 teaspoon salt in a colander. Place the colander on a plate and refrigerate to drain off excess juices, 30 to 60 minutes, the longer the better. Rinse well and pat the cucumbers dry with paper towels. Transfer to a bowl, add the yogurt and mint and mix well. Season with salt (be careful, as the cucumbers are salty) and pepper. Refrigerate until ready to serve.

2. Have ready 4 long metal skewers. Toss the lamb in a medium bowl with 2 teaspoons of the oil to coat; season with salt, sprinkle with the spice rub, and toss again. Toss the red pepper squares and zucchini pieces in another bowl with the remaining 2 teaspoons of oil, season with salt and pepper, and toss. Thread 4 lamb cubes, 4 red pepper squares, and 2 zucchini pieces onto each skewer, alternating the ingredients as you wish. Cover and let stand at room temperature while building the fire. (The kebabs can be prepared up to 1 day ahead, covered and refrigerated. Remove from the refrigerator 30 minutes before grilling.)

3. Build a charcoal fire in an outdoor grill for direct high grilling (see page 8) and let burn until the coals are almost completely covered with white ash.

4. Lightly oil the grill grate. Place the lamb on the grill and cover. Grill, turning occasionally, until the lamb is browned on all sides and feels somewhat firm when pressed, about 6 minutes for medium-rare meat, or longer if desired. Transfer to a large platter.

5. Let the kebabs stand for 3 to 5 minutes. Slide the meat and vegetables off each skewer onto each dinner plate. Serve hot, with the chilled raita passed on the side.

KEBABS

Kebabs have long been a favorite dish for entertaining, but there are some tricks. First, long metal skewers are a wise investment, as no matter how you soak and protect bamboo skewers, they tend to burn. And the flat blades on the metal skewers stop the food from spinning like a merry-go-round when the kebabs are turned. Also, choose sturdy vegetables that will stand up to grilling—tomatoes turn to mush by the time the lamb is cooked, and eggplant may be underdone.

Because the lamb is in small cubes, you will have to rely on your senses and experience to check for doneness, as a thermometer cannot be inserted accurately into the meat. See When Is It Done?, on page 13, for details.

MARRAKESH LAMB SKEWERS WITH LEMON COUSCOUS SALAD

MAKES 4 SERVINGS
Grilling Method: Direct High

The **exotic spicing** of these **ground lamb kebabs** will arouse the dullest appetite. The ground lamb mixture is shaped onto metal skewers (the ones with the flat blades work best) and seared on the grill. Thanks to ground onions in the lamb mixture, these turn out so moist that you won't need a sauce.

COUSCOUS SALAD

½ TEASPOON SALT

1 CUP COUSCOUS

2 TABLESPOONS FRESH LEMON JUICE

2 TABLESPOONS EXTRA-VIRGIN OLIVE OIL

⅓ CUP FINELY CHOPPED RED BELL PEPPER

2 TABLESPOONS CHOPPED FRESH MINT

2 POUNDS GROUND LAMB

1 MEDIUM ONION, SHREDDED ON THE LARGE HOLES OF A BOX GRATER

4 GARLIC CLOVES, MINCED

1 TABLESPOON TOMATO PASTE

2 TEASPOONS SWEET PAPRIKA, PREFERABLY HUNGARIAN

1 TEASPOON SALT

1 TEASPOON GROUND CUMIN

½ TEASPOON GROUND GINGER

½ TEASPOON FRESHLY GROUND BLACK PEPPER

1. To make the salad, bring 1½ cups water and the salt to a boil in a small saucepan. Stir in the couscous, remove from the heat, and cover. Let stand for 5 minutes. Transfer to a medium bowl and fluff the couscous with the tines of a fork. Stir in the lemon juice and oil, then the red bell pepper and mint. Let stand at room temperature until ready to serve.

2. Mix the ground lamb, onion, garlic, tomato paste, paprika, salt, cumin, ginger, and pepper together in a medium bowl. Divide the mixture into 16 equal portions. Shape 4 portions onto each skewer, shaping each portion in a thick cylinder about 1½ inches long. Cover and let stand at room temperature while lighting the grill. (The skewers can be prepared up to 8 hours ahead, covered and refrigerated. Remove from the refrigerator 30 minutes before grilling.)

3. Build a charcoal fire in an outdoor grill for direct high grilling (see page 8) and let burn until the coals are almost completely covered with white ash. Be sure to leave a 2- to 3-inch-wide perimeter around the mound of coals.

4. Lightly oil the grill grate. Place the lamb on the grill and cover. Grill, turning occasionally, until the lamb is browned on all sides and feels somewhat firm when pressed, about 6 minutes for medium-rare meat, or longer if desired. Depending on the fat content of the lamb, you may have a fair amount of flare-ups. If they become excessive, move the kebabs to the cooler area around the coals. Transfer to a large platter.

5. Let the skewers stand for 3 to 5 minutes. Spoon equal amounts of the salad onto 4 dinner plates. Slide the meat off each skewer onto the salad and serve.

LAMB RIB CHOPS WITH MINT BUTTER

MAKES 4 SERVINGS
Grilling Method: Direct High

When grilling pricey cuts of meat, it is best to let the meat speak for itself, without rubs, marinades, or smoky accents to cloak the flavor. Here, lamb rib chops, which include the tenderest part of the lamb, are served simply grilled with **a dollop of mint butter.** The butter should be quite soft so it melts readily when it comes into contact with the meat. Add a simple side dish of steamed sugar snap peas and perhaps some roasted potatoes, and you have **one classy dinner.**

MINT BUTTER

8 TABLESPOONS (1 STICK) UNSALTED BUTTER, SOFTENED

2 TABLESPOONS FINELY CHOPPED FRESH MINT

1 TEASPOON FRESH LEMON JUICE

1 GARLIC CLOVE, CRUSHED THROUGH A PRESS

SALT AND FRESHLY GROUND BLACK PEPPER TO TASTE

TWELVE 2½-OUNCE LAMB RIB CHOPS, CUT 1 INCH THICK

SALT AND FRESHLY GROUND BLACK PEPPER TO TASTE

LAMB AU JUS (PAGE 109), OPTIONAL

1. To make the mint butter, mash the butter, mint, lemon juice, and garlic clove together with a rubber spatula in a small bowl. Season with salt and pepper. Set aside at room temperature until ready to serve. (The butter can be made up to 1 week ahead, covered and refrigerated. Bring the butter to room temperature before serving.)

2. Season the lamb chops with salt and pepper and let stand at room temperature while building the fire.

3. Build a charcoal fire in an outdoor grill for direct high grilling (see page 8) and let burn until the coals are almost completely covered with white ash.

4. Lightly oil the grill grate. Place the lamb on the grill and cover. Grill, turning occasionally, until the lamb is browned on all sides and feels somewhat firm when pressed, about 5 minutes for medium-rare meat. It is more reliable to use your sense of touch and sight to judge the doneness, as it is difficult to insert a thermometer into a rib chop. If you want to try anyway, insert an instant-read thermometer horizontally at the center of a chop; it should read 125°F for medium-rare, or longer if desired.

5. Transfer 3 chops to each of 4 dinner plates. Spoon a couple of tablespoons of the au jus around the chops, if using. Top the chops with a dollop of the butter and serve immediately.

RACK OF LAMB WITH TAPENADE CRUST

MAKES 4 SERVINGS
Grilling Method: Banked

Like rosemary and mint, **olives are perfect partnered with lamb.**
Tapenade is a French olive paste that can be served slathered onto toasted bread as a snack, but it makes one *magnifique* coating for rack of lamb, too. Tapenade includes a dash of anchovy paste, but it will taste uniquely salty, not fishy. The lamb is browned before adding the crust to ensure deep caramelized flavors.

TAPENADE

2 GARLIC CLOVES, CRUSHED UNDER A KNIFE AND PEELED

1 CUP PITTED KALAMATA OR OTHER MEDITERRANEAN BLACK OLIVES

1 TEASPOON DIJON MUSTARD

1 TEASPOON ANCHOVY PASTE

½ TEASPOON HERBES DE PROVENCE, OR ¼ TEASPOON EACH DRIED ROSEMARY AND THYME

¼ TEASPOON CRUSHED HOT RED PEPPER

2 TABLESPOONS EXTRA-VIRGIN OLIVE OIL

TWO 1¼ POUND RACKS OF LAMB, TRIMMED OF EXCESS FAT (SEE NOTE)

SALT AND FRESHLY GROUND BLACK PEPPER TO TASTE

⅔ CUP PANKO (JAPANESE BREAD CRUMBS) OR FRESH BREAD CRUMBS

2 TEASPOONS EXTRA-VIRGIN OLIVE OIL

LAMB AU JUS (PAGE 109), OPTIONAL

1. To make the tapenade, with the machine running, drop the garlic through the feed tube of a food processor fitted with the metal blade, to chop it. Add the olives, mustard, anchovy paste, herbes de Provence, and hot pepper, and pulse to chop the olives. With the machine running, add the oil. Transfer to a small bowl and set aside. (The tapenade can be made up to 2 weeks ahead, covered and refrigerated.)

2. As the tapenade is highly seasoned, season the lamb lightly with salt and pepper. To keep the bones from burning, cover the row of bones with a strip of aluminum foil. (This sounds fussy, but you'll be glad you did it in the long run.) Cover and let stand at room temperature while building the fire.

3. Build a charcoal fire in an outdoor grill for banked grilling (see page 10) and let burn until the coals are almost completely covered with white ash.

4. Lightly oil the grill grate. Place the lamb, meaty sides down, over the hotter area of the grill and cover. Grill, turning once, until browned on both sides, about 3½ minutes. Transfer the lamb to a platter, meaty side facing up.

5. Spread the meaty side of one lamb rack with half of the tapenade. Sprinkle evenly with ⅓ cup of the panko, pressing the crumbs firmly onto the tapenade. Drizzle with 1 teaspoon of the oil. Repeat with the remaining lamb, tapenade, panko, and oil.

6. Return the lamb to the grill, placing it over the cooler area. Cover and grill until an instant-read thermometer inserted horizontally through the "eye" of the rack into the center reads 125°F, about 15 minutes for medium-rare, or longer, if desired.

7. Transfer to a carving board with a well and let stand 5 minutes. Cut between each rib. Place 4 ribs on each of 4 dinner plates and drizzle with the carving juices (spoon 2 table-spoons of the lamb au jus, if using, around each serving), and serve hot.

Note: Be sure that the chine bone of the lamb has been prepared for carving. It should be nicked between each rib by the butcher with a meat saw. Often, imported Cryovac-packed racks of lamb lack this feature, making it impossible to cut the rack into chops for easier serving.

PANKO

These crisp, flaky Japanese bread crumbs can be found at Asian grocers and many supermarkets. They make especially crunchy crusts for dishes like rack of lamb or meat patties, and can be used in any recipe that calls for dried bread crumbs. However, if you need to use a substitute, use fresh bread crumbs made from a crusty roll in a food processor or blender, as these crumbs will best simulate the fluffiness of panko.

LAMB PITA BURGERS WITH CHOPPED GREEK SALAD

MAKES 4 SERVINGS
Grilling Method: Pocket

Beef is safe in its position as America's favorite burger. But if more people taste these lamb **burgers with Greek influences,** beef might have cause for worry. The **fresh-tasting salad** acts as a kind of condiment, but if you like, mix ½ cup plain yogurt with 1 garlic clove, and add a spoonful or two to your pita.

CHOPPED GREEK SALAD

1 TABLESPOON RED WINE VINEGAR

¼ TEASPOON DRIED OREGANO

SALT AND FRESHLY GROUND BLACK PEPPER TO TASTE

¼ CUP EXTRA-VIRGIN OLIVE OIL

1 CUP PEELED, SEEDED, AND ¼-INCH-DICE CUCUMBER

1 MEDIUM TOMATO, SEEDED AND CUT INTO ¼ INCH DICE

⅓ CUP ¼-INCH-DICE RED BELL PEPPER

3 TABLESPOONS CHOPPED PITTED KALAMATA OLIVES

½ CUP (2 OUNCES) CRUMBLED FETA CHEESE

1½ POUNDS GROUND LAMB

1 TEASPOON SALT

½ TEASPOON FRESHLY GROUND BLACK PEPPER

4 POCKET-STYLE PITA BREADS, 1 INCH CUT FROM THE TOP OF EACH

1. To make the salad, whisk the vinegar, oregano, salt, and pepper in a medium bowl. Gradually whisk in the oil. Add the cucumber, tomato, red pepper, and olives and mix well. Fold in the cheese. Set aside until ready to serve.

2. Mix the ground lamb, salt, and pepper in a medium bowl. Gently shape into 4 oval-shaped burgers, about 5 × 3 inches each. Cover and set aside at room temperature while building the fire.

3. Build a charcoal fire in an outdoor grill for pocket grilling (see page 11) and let burn until the coals are almost completely covered with white ash.

4. Place the lamb burgers on the grill and cover. Grill, turning occasionally, until browned on both sides and the lamb feels somewhat firm when pressed in the center, about 6 minutes for medium-rare, or longer, if desired. If the lamb gives off fat and makes flare-ups, move the burgers to the empty pockets in the coals and continue grilling. During the last minute or so, place the pita on the grill and grill, turning once, until lightly toasted.

5. Place a burger in each pita and add equal portions of the salad. Serve hot.

POMEGRANATE-MARINATED LAMB STEAKS WITH PITA AND VEGETABLE SALAD

MAKES 4 SERVINGS
Grilling Method: Banked

These grilled lamb steaks are redolent of Mediterranean flavors. The **pomegranate** marinade is just the beginning, and the dish is rounded out with *fattoush*, a vegetable salad accented with **olives, feta, and crunchy pita bread chips.** Leg of lamb shows up occasionally in the supermarket case, or a cooperative butcher will cut the steaks from an entire leg. Use this combination for other lamb cuts, from butterflied leg of lamb to rib chops.

FOUR 12-OUNCE LEG OF LAMB STEAKS, CUT ABOUT ¾ INCH THICK

POMEGRANATE MARINADE (PAGE 31)

PITA AND VEGETABLE SALAD FATTOUSH

2 TABLESPOONS FRESH LEMON JUICE

SALT AND FRESHLY GROUND BLACK PEPPER TO TASTE

½ CUP EXTRA-VIRGIN OLIVE OIL

1 ROMAINE LETTUCE HEART, TORN INTO BITE-SIZE PIECES

1 MEDIUM TOMATO, SEEDED AND CUT INTO ½-INCH DICE

1 KIRBY CUCUMBER, SCRUBBED AND CUT INTO ¼-INCH DICE

¼ CUP CHOPPED RED ONION

3 TABLESPOONS CHOPPED FRESH PARSLEY

⅓ CUP PITTED AND CHOPPED KALAMATA OLIVES

½ CUP CRUMBLED FETA CHEESE, PREFERABLY IMPORTED

1 PITA BREAD, SPLIT IN HALF HORIZONTALLY

1.   Divide the lamb and marinade among two 1-gallon resealable plastic bags. Let stand at room temperature for 1 hour, or refrigerate for up to 3 hours. If refrigerated, let stand at room temperature for 1 hour before grilling.

2. Build a charcoal fire in an outdoor grill for banked grilling (see page 10) and let burn until the coals are almost completely covered with white ash.

3. Meanwhile, to prepare the fattoush, whisk the lemon juice, salt, and pepper in a small bowl. Gradually whisk in the oil. Combine the lettuce, tomato, cucumber, red onion, parsley, olives, and feta in a medium bowl. Set the lemon vinaigrette and salad aside.

4. Place the pita bread over the hottest area of the grill and grill uncovered, turning occasionally, until toasted, about 1 minute. Set aside to cool.

5. Lightly oil the grill grate. Remove the lamb from the marinade. Place the lamb steaks over the hottest area of the grill and cover. Cook until the underside is browned, about 2 minutes. Turn, cover, and grill the other side, about 2 minutes longer. Move to the cooler side of the grill and cover. Grill, turning once, until the lamb feels somewhat firm when pressed, about 4 minutes longer for medium-rare, or longer if desired. Transfer each lamb steak to a dinner plate.

6. Tear the pita bread into bite-size pieces and add to the salad. Add the lemon vinaigrette to the salad and mix well. Serve with the lamb.

PORK

SPICE-RUBBED PORK CHOPS WITH HONEY GLAZE AND APPLE SLAW

GRILLING CLASSIC

MAKES 4 SERVINGS
Grilling Method: Banked

One of the most common questions about outdoor cooking concerns how to grill **moist, flavorful** pork chops. Start by choosing the right chops—¾ to 1 inch thick—as thin ones overcook easily, and overcooking is the enemy of pork chops. Grill them just until the meat feels firm and springs back when pressed in the center. Banked grilling helps the chops cook at a moderate temperature and retain their juices.

APPLE–POPPY SEED SLAW

½ CUP MAYONNAISE

1½ TABLESPOONS CIDER VINEGAR

1½ TABLESPOONS THAWED FROZEN APPLE
JUICE CONCENTRATE

ONE 1-POUND BAG COLESLAW MIX

1 GRANNY SMITH APPLE, CORED AND
SHREDDED ON THE LARGE HOLES OF A
BOX GRATER

2 SCALLIONS, WHITE AND GREEN PARTS,
FINELY CHOPPED

1 TABLESPOON POPPY SEEDS

SALT AND FRESHLY GROUND BLACK PEPPER
TO TASTE

FOUR 9-OUNCE CENTER-CUT PORK CHOPS,
CUT ABOUT 1 INCH THICK

SALT TO TASTE

2 TABLESPOONS THE ULTIMATE SPICE RUB
(PAGE 34)

¼ CUP HONEY, WARMED UNTIL FLUID

1. To make the slaw, whisk the mayonnaise, vinegar, and apple juice concentrate together in a medium bowl. Add the cole slaw mix, apple, and scallions, and mix. Add the poppy seeds and mix again. Season with salt and pepper. Cover and refrigerate until ready to serve. (The slaw can be made up to 1 day ahead, covered and refrigerated.)

2. Season the pork chops with salt. Sprinkle with the rub. Cover and let stand at room temperature while lighting the coals.

3. Build a charcoal fire in an outdoor grill for banked grilling (page 10) and let burn until the coals are almost completely covered with white ash.

4. Lightly oil the grill grate. Place the pork chops over the hotter area of the grill. Cover and cook, turning once, until the undersides are seared with grill marks, about 2 minutes per side. Move to the cooler area of the grill and cover. Grill, turning occasionally, until the meat feels firm and springs back when pressed in the center, about 15 minutes for medium-well meat. It is more reliable to use your sense of touch and sight to judge the doneness, as it is difficult to insert a thermometer into a pork chop. If you want to try anyway, insert an instant-read thermometer horizontally at the center of a chop; it should read 150°F for medium-well. During the last few minutes, brush the chops on both sides with the honey. Transfer the pork chops to a platter.

5. Spoon equal amounts of the slaw onto each of 4 dinner plates. Top each with a pork chop and serve hot.

BEER-BRINED PORK CHOPS WITH HOT POTATO SALAD

MAKES 4 SERVINGS
Grilling Method: Banked

Brining is a popular way to add moisture to pork chops, and an excellent one, too, if you keep a few points in mind. Before brining, be sure that your pork has not been "enhanced" with sodium additives (it should say so clearly on the package, but ask the butcher if you are unsure), or your chops will be unpalatably salty. Allow **at least 4 hours** to brine the chops, but no longer than 8 hours, as a longer soak will not do the chops any good. The bourbon brine is great here, too.

FOUR 9-OUNCE CENTER-CUT PORK CHOPS, CUT ABOUT 1 INCH THICK

BEER AND MUSTARD BRINE (PAGE 44) OR APPLE CIDER AND BOURBON BRINE (PAGE 42)

HOT POTATO SALAD

2 POUNDS RED-SKIN POTATOES

3 STRIPS BACON

3 TABLESPOONS WHITE WINE VINEGAR

1 TEASPOON GRAINY DIJON-STYLE MUSTARD

1 TEASPOON SUGAR

½ CUP VEGETABLE OIL

2 SCALLIONS, WHITE AND GREEN PARTS, CHOPPED

SALT AND FRESHLY GROUND BLACK PEPPER TO TASTE

1. Place the pork chops in a medium bowl and add the brine. Cover and refrigerate for at least 4 and up to 8 hours, no longer.

2. To make the potato salad, place the potatoes in a medium saucepan and add enough salted cold water to cover. Bring to a boil over high heat. Reduce the heat to medium and simmer, uncovered, until the potatoes are tender when pierced with the tip of a sharp knife, about 30 minutes. Drain.

3. Meanwhile, place the bacon in a large skillet and cook over medium heat until browned and crisp, about 10 minutes. Transfer the bacon to paper towels, reserving the fat in the skillet. Cool, coarsely chop, and reserve the bacon.

4. Whisk the vinegar, mustard, sugar, and oil into the reserved bacon fat. Slice the potatoes (do not peel) into ¼-inch-thick rounds and transfer to a medium bowl. Add the vinegar mixture and scallions and mix well. Season with salt and pepper. Set the salad aside at room temperature until ready to serve.

5. Build a charcoal fire in an outdoor grill for banked grilling (page 10) and let burn until the coals are almost completely covered with white ash.

6. Lightly oil the grill grate. Place the pork chops over the hotter area of the grill. Cover and cook, turning once, until the undersides are seared with grill marks, about 2 minutes per side. Move to the cooler area of the grill and cover. Grill, turning occasionally, until the meat feels firm and springs back when pressed in the center, about 15 minutes for medium-well meat. It is more reliable to use your sense of touch and sight to judge the doneness, as it is difficult to insert a thermometer into a pork chop. If you want to try anyway, insert an instant-read thermometer horizontally at the center of a chop; it should read 150°F for medium-well.

7. Sprinkle the reserved bacon over the potato salad. Spoon equal amounts of the salad onto each of 4 dinner plates. Top each with a pork chop and serve hot.

JAMAICAN JERK PORK CHOPS WITH ORANGE YAMS

MAKES 4 SERVINGS
Grilling Method: Banked

Jerk seasoning went from something you had only when **vacationing in Jamaica** to a familiar flavor on your local supermarket shelves. Use Scotch bonnet or habañero chiles for authentic Caribbean flavor—the former is larger than the latter, but both look like tam-o'-shanters and are very spicy. It is best to make the jerk with only half of a chile, taste, and then decide if you are **brave enough to add more.**

JERK PORK CHOPS

2 GARLIC CLOVES

6 SCALLIONS, WHITE AND GREEN PARTS, COARSELY CHOPPED

1/2 SCOTCH BONNET OR HABAÑERO CHILE, SEEDS AND RIBS DISCARDED, COARSELY CHOPPED

2 TABLESPOONS SOY SAUCE

1 TABLESPOON CIDER VINEGAR

2 TEASPOONS DRIED THYME

1 TEASPOON GROUND ALLSPICE

1/4 TEASPOON SALT

FOUR 9-OUNCE CENTER-CUT PORK CHOPS, CUT 1 INCH THICK

ORANGE YAMS

8 TABLESPOONS UNSALTED BUTTER, SOFTENED

GRATED ZEST OF 1 LARGE NAVEL ORANGE

2 LARGE YAMS, PEELED, AND CUT INTO 1/2-INCH-THICK ROUNDS

1/2 CUP FRESH ORANGE JUICE

SALT AND FRESHLY GROUND PEPPER TO TASTE

1. To make the jerk pork chops, with the machine running, drop the garlic through the feed tube of a food processor fitted with the metal chopping blade. Add the scallions and chile and pulse until chopped. Add the soy sauce, vinegar, thyme, allspice, and salt, and process until smooth. Place the jerk paste into a 1-gallon resealable plastic bag and add the chops. Close the bag and let stand at room temperature for 1 hour. (The pork and jerk can be refrigerated for up to 12 hours. Remove from the refrigerator 1 hour before grilling.)

2. To prepare the yams, tear off four 12-inch lengths of aluminum foil. Mix the butter and orange zest in a small bowl until combined. Spread one-fourth of the yams in the center of 1 foil square and top with 2 tablespoons of the butter mixture and 2 tablespoons of orange juice. Season with salt and pepper. Fold the top and bottom of the foil to meet in the center, and pleat the top and sides closed. Repeat with the remaining yams, butter, and foil. Set aside at room temperature while building the fire.

3. Build a charcoal fire in an outdoor grill for banked grilling (page 10) and let burn until the coals are almost completely covered with white ash.

4. Lightly oil the grill grate. Place the yams in their packets over the hottest area of the grill, cover, and cook for 5 minutes. Move the packets to the cooler side of the grill and add the pork chops to the hottest area. Cover and grill, turning once, until the chops are browned on both sides, about 6 minutes. Move the chops to the cooler side (move the yams to the edge of the grill, if you are short on room), cover, and grill until the meat feels firm and springs back when pressed in the center, about 20 minutes more for medium-well meat. As it is difficult to insert a meat thermometer into a pork chop, it is more reliable to use your sense of touch and sight to judge the doneness. If you want to try anyway, insert an instant-read thermometer horizontally at the center of a chop; it should read 150°F for medium-well. Transfer the pork chops to a platter. Open a foil packet and check the yams for doneness—they should be tender when pierced with the tip of a sharp knife.

5. Place a pork chop on each of 4 dinner plates. Open each foil packet and pour the yams and sauce onto each plate. Serve hot.

HERBED PORK TENDERLOIN WITH PORTOBELLOS

MAKES 4 SERVINGS
Grilling Method: Banked

One of the most important techniques with grilling is learning to cook different parts of a meal on the grill at the same time. Here, pork tenderloin cooks alongside **hearty portobello** mushrooms to make an easy home meal that looks like a professional chef prepared it.

¼ CUP OLIVE OIL

2 GARLIC CLOVES, CHOPPED

1 POUND BONELESS PORK TENDERLOIN, SILVER SKIN TRIMMED AWAY

4 LARGE PORTOBELLO MUSHROOMS, WASHED, STEMS REMOVED

1 TABLESPOON HERBES DE PROVENCE, OR 1 TEASPOON EACH DRIED ROSEMARY, THYME, AND BASIL

½ TEASPOON SALT

½ TEASPOON FRESHLY GROUND BLACK PEPPER

4 TEASPOONS BALSAMIC VINEGAR

CHOPPED FRESH ROSEMARY OR SAGE, FOR GARNISH

1. Build a charcoal fire in an outdoor grill for banked grilling (page 10) and let burn until the coals are almost completely covered with white ash.

2. Heat the oil and garlic in a small saucepan over medium-low heat until the garlic is surrounded by tiny bubbles, about 6 minutes. Transfer to a small bowl. Brush the pork and mushrooms with the garlic oil; reserve the remaining garlic oil. Mix the herbes de Provence, salt, and pepper together and rub the herb mixture all over the pork.

3. Place the pork over the hotter area of the grill and cover the grill. Grill the pork, turning occasionally, until seared on all sides, about 5 minutes. Move to the cooler side of the grill and place the mushrooms next to them. Brush again with the remaining garlic oil. Grill, turning occasionally, until an instant-read thermometer inserted into the center of the pork reads 150°F and the mushrooms are tender, 12 to 15 minutes. Transfer the pork and mushrooms to a platter.

4. Place a mushroom cap on each of 4 dinner plates. Let the pork stand for a few minutes, then cut into ½-inch-thick slices. Fan equal amounts of the sliced pork over the mushrooms. Drizzle each with 1 teaspoon of vinegar, sprinkle with the fresh herbs, and serve hot.

MORE IDEAS FOR PORK TENDERLOIN

Use as a template the banked cooking method used in this recipe, which browns the meat over high heat then cooks it more gently over low coals. Here are some ideas for other flavor combinations for this versatile cut.

SPICE-RUBBED PORK TENDERLOIN: Rub each 1-pound pork tenderloin with 1 tablespoon of The Ultimate Spice Rub (page 34), Tex-Mex Rub (page 36), or Mediterranean Herb Paste (page 39).

MARINATED PORK TENDERLOIN: Marinate the tenderloins in Herbed Red Wine Marinade (page 24), Cuban Citrus Marinade (page 27), or Teriyaki Marinade (page 30).

GLAZED PORK TENDERLOIN: A few minutes before removing the tenderloin from the grill, brush with a barbecue sauce to complement the flavor of the employed spice rub, marinade, or brine. Try All-American Barbecue Sauce (page 18) with The Ultimate Spice Rub, or Big Apple Barbecue Sauce (page 18) with Small Batch Apple Cider Brine (page 42).

PORK SATAY WITH PEANUT SAUCE

MAKES 4 SERVINGS
Grilling Method: Direct High

Along with kebabs and souvlaki, satay is a member of the **skewered food family,** but the meat is usually cut into strips, rather than cubes, making it especially quick cooking. The marinade and the all-important peanut dipping sauce for this Southeast Asian specialty have plenty of ingredients, but they come together quickly, too. When grilling, be sure that the exposed wooden skewers are **not directly over the coals,** or they will scorch.

PORK SATAY

¼ CUP VEGETABLE OIL

2 TABLESPOONS THAI OR VIETNAMESE FISH SAUCE

2 TABLESPOONS FINELY CHOPPED SHALLOT

1 TABLESPOON LIGHT OR DARK BROWN SUGAR

2 GARLIC CLOVES, FINELY CHOPPED

2 TEASPOONS PEELED AND FINELY CHOPPED FRESH GINGER

1 TEASPOON MADRAS-STYLE CURRY POWDER

¼ TEASPOON CRUSHED HOT RED PEPPER

1 POUND CENTER-CUT BONELESS PORK LOIN, SURFACE FAT TRIMMED

24 WOODEN SKEWERS, SOAKED IN WATER FOR AT LEAST 30 MINUTES, DRAINED

PEANUT SAUCE

1 TABLESPOON VEGETABLE OIL

2 TABLESPOONS FINELY CHOPPED SHALLOT

1 GARLIC CLOVE, FINELY CHOPPED

½ CUP CHUNKY PEANUT BUTTER

½ CUP CANNED COCONUT MILK

2 TEASPOONS HOISIN SAUCE

2 TEASPOONS THAI OR VIETNAMESE SAUCE

⅛ TEASPOON CRUSHED HOT RED PEPPER

1. To make the pork satay, whisk together the oil, fish sauce, shallot, brown sugar, garlic, ginger, curry powder, and red pepper until combined.

2. Cut the pork loin crosswise into ¼-inch-thick slices. Cut each slice lengthwise into 3 wide strips. Lightly pound each strip to ⅛-inch thickness. Place the pork strips in a 1-gallon resealable plastic bag, add the marinade, and close the bag. Let stand at room temperature while building the fire, or refrigerate for up to 8 hours. Drain the pork strips and thread 1 strip on each drained skewer.

3. Just before building the fire, make the peanut sauce: heat the oil in a small saucepan over medium heat. Add the shallot and cook, stirring often, until softened, about 2 minutes. Stir in the garlic and cook until fragrant, about 1 minute. Stir in the peanut butter, coconut milk, ¼ cup water, hoisin sauce, fish sauce, and hot pepper and bring to a simmer. Reduce the heat to medium-low and simmer, whisking often, for 5 minutes to blend the flavors. Cover and keep warm. (The sauce can be made up to 2 days ahead, cooled, covered, and refrigerated. Reheat gently, whisking often, before serving.)

4. Build a charcoal fire in an outdoor grill for direct high grilling (page 8) and let burn until the coals are almost completely covered with white ash. Do not spread out the coals, but leave them heaped in the center with a 2- to 3-inch-wide border around them.

5. Lightly oil the grill grate. Place the skewers on the grill in a spoke pattern, with the meat over the coals but the skewers over the border around the coals. Grill uncovered (if covered, the heat could scorch the skewers), turning once, until the pork is browned on both sides and the meat shows no sign of pink when pierced with the tip of a knife, about 5 minutes. Serve hot with the warmed peanut sauce.

CUBAN PORK LOIN WITH BLACK BEANS AND RICE

MAKES 6 SERVINGS
Grilling Method: Indirect High

It's no secret that meat cooked **on the bone has the best flavor.** On the other hand, boneless loin pork roasts are in every supermarket. A long soak in a **zesty Cuban marinade** takes this roast out of the ordinary. When making a side dish, you can't improve on the traditional accompaniment of black beans and rice. Converted rice cooks into separate grains, but you can use regular long-grain rice, if you prefer.

ONE 3-POUND BONELESS CENTER-CUT LOIN PORK ROAST

CUBAN CITRUS MARINADE (PAGE 27)

BLACK BEANS AND RICE

1 1/4 CUPS CONVERTED LONG-GRAIN RICE

2 1/2 CUPS CANNED REDUCED-SODIUM CHICKEN BROTH

1/2 TEASPOON SALT

1 TABLESPOON OLIVE OIL

3 OUNCES HARD, SPICY SMOKED SAUSAGE, SUCH AS CHORIZO, CASING REMOVED, CUT INTO 1/4-INCH DICE

1 MEDIUM ONION, CHOPPED

1/2 CUP CHOPPED GREEN BELL PEPPER

2 GARLIC CLOVES, FINELY CHOPPED

ONE 15- TO 19-OUNCE CAN BLACK BEANS, DRAINED AND RINSED

2 TABLESPOONS CHOPPED FRESH CILANTRO

1. Place the roast in a 1-gallon resealable plastic bag and add the marinade. Close the bag and refrigerate for at least 4 and up to 8 hours.

2. Build a charcoal fire in an outdoor grill for indirect high grilling (page 10) and let burn until the coals are almost completely covered with white ash.

3. Drain the pork and discard the marinade. Lightly oil the grill grate. Pour 1 cup water into a drip pan. Place the pork over the drip pan and cover. Grill until an instant-read thermometer inserted in the center reads 150°F, about 1 hour.

4. Meanwhile, make the black beans and rice. Bring the rice, broth, and salt to a boil in a medium saucepan over high heat. Reduce the heat to low and cover. Simmer until the rice absorbs the liquid and is tender, about 20 minutes. Remove from the heat and let stand 5 minutes.

5. Heat the oil in a large skillet over medium heat. Add the chorizo and cook, stirring often, until the chorizo is lightly browned, about 5 minutes. Add the onion and bell pepper and cook, stirring often, until softened, about 3 minutes. Stir in the garlic and cook until fragrant, about 1 minute. Add the black beans and ¼ cup water. Cook, stirring often, until the beans are heated through, about 5 minutes. Stir in the rice. Transfer to a serving bowl, sprinkle with the cilantro, and cover to keep warm.

6. Transfer the pork roast to a serving platter. Let stand for 10 minutes, then slice. Serve hot with the black beans and rice passed on the side.

PORK LOIN PORCHETTA WITH CANNELLINI AND TOMATO SALAD

MAKES 6 SERVINGS
Grilling Method: Indirect High

At every Tuscan outdoor market, there is always a vendor grilling **herb-stuffed,** spit-roasted pork all morning long, and quite a big deal is made when the meat is finally ready to be served. While Italians often use pork shoulder, this method can be applied to bone-in **pork loin with great results.** The blade end has a bit more fat and flavor, but a center cut is fine, too. If you wish, toss some soaked and drained oak chips on the coals to give the meat even more Italian flair.

ONE 3¾-POUND PORK LOIN ROAST WITH BONES, PREFERABLY FROM THE BLADE END

1 TABLESPOON EXTRA-VIRGIN OLIVE OIL

2 TEASPOONS CHOPPED FRESH ROSEMARY

2 TEASPOONS CHOPPED FRESH THYME

2 TEASPOONS CHOPPED FRESH SAGE

1 TEASPOON FENNEL SEED, COARSELY GROUND IN A SPICE GRINDER OR A MORTAR

2 GARLIC CLOVES, CRUSHED THROUGH A PRESS

1 TEASPOON SALT

½ TEASPOON FRESHLY GROUND BLACK PEPPER

1 CUP DRY WHITE WINE

CANNELLINI AND TOMATO SALAD

1½ TABLESPOONS RED WINE VINEGAR

⅓ CUP PLUS 1 TABLESPOON EXTRA-VIRGIN OLIVE OIL

TWO 15- TO 19-OUNCE CANS CANNELLINI (WHITE KIDNEY) BEANS, DRAINED AND RINSED

1 PINT GRAPE OR CHERRY TOMATOES, CUT IN HALVES LENGTHWISE

1 SMALL RED ONION, CHOPPED

1½ TEASPOONS FINELY CHOPPED SAGE

1½ TEASPOONS FINELY CHOPPED ROSEMARY

SALT AND FRESHLY GROUND PEPPER TO TASTE

1. Using a sharp thin knife, trim the outer surface fat from the pork. Pierce 10 evenly spaced slits, about ½ inch deep, in the pork. Mix together the oil, rosemary, thyme, sage, fennel, garlic, salt, and pepper in a small bowl. Stuff the slits with most of the herb paste, and rub any remaining paste over the pork. Cover and let stand at room temperature while building the fire.

2. Build a charcoal fire in an outdoor grill for indirect high grilling (page 10) and let burn until the coals are almost completely covered with white ash. You will not need a drip pan.

3. Place the pork, meaty side up, in a disposable aluminum foil pan that will hold it comfortably. You will not need a meat rack, as the bones form a natural one. Place the pork on the empty side of the grill. Pour the wine over the pork and cover. Grill until an instant-read thermometer inserted in the center of the pork reads 150°F, about 1¼ hours. During this period, occasionally baste the pork with the wine in the pan. After about 45 minutes, add 6 briquets to the coals to maintain the temperature.

4. Meanwhile, make the salad. Whisk the vinegar in a medium bowl and gradually whisk in the oil. Add the beans, tomatoes, onion, sage, and rosemary, and mix well. Season with salt and pepper. Cover and let stand at room temperature until ready to serve. (The bean salad can be made up to 1 day ahead, covered and refrigerated. Bring to room temperature before serving.)

5. Transfer the pork to a platter and let stand for 10 minutes. Carve the roast and serve hot, with the bean salad.

BACKYARD BARBECUED RIBS

GRILLING CLASSIC

MAKES 4 TO 6 SERVINGS
Grilling Method: Indirect Low

How many times have you seen a grill cook struggle with barbecued ribs, fighting flare-ups as he cooks the meat directly over the coals? This scenario is easily fixed with the patient cooking of indirect heat, and the ribs pick up **lots of smoky flavor** in the bargain. The initial cooking can be done well ahead of serving—just put the ribs back on the grill for their final glazing. **A metal rib rack** is a great investment, holding more ribs than if they were placed flat.

5 POUNDS SPARERIBS

1¾ TEASPOONS SALT

⅓ CUP THE ULTIMATE SPICE RUB (PAGE 34)

4 OR 5 HANDFULS OF HICKORY WOOD CHIPS, SOAKED IN WATER TO COVER FOR AT LEAST 30 MINUTES, DRAINED

ONE 12-OUNCE CAN COLA SODA OR GINGER ALE

2 CUPS ALL-AMERICAN BARBECUE SAUCE (PAGE 18)

1. Season the ribs all over with the salt, then sprinkle with the spice rub. Cover and let stand while building the fire.

2. Build a charcoal fire in an outdoor grill for indirect low grilling (page 9) and let burn until the coals are almost completely covered with white ash.

3. Lightly oil the grill grate. Sprinkle a handful of chips on the coals. Add 2 cups water to a drip pan. Place a metal rib rack over the drip pan. Arrange the ribs in the rack (they will be floppy, but will firm up as they cook) and cover. Grill until the ribs are fork-tender, 2½ to 3 hours. After 45 minutes, and every 45 minutes or so after that, toss another handful of chips on the coals, add 6 briquets to the coals to maintain the temperature, and baste with a trickle of the soda to moisten the spice rub. Transfer the ribs to a platter. (The ribs can be prepared to this point up to 8 hours ahead, cooled, covered, and refrigerated.)

4. Remove the rib rack from the grill. Remove the grill grate from the grill and add about 3 pounds of charcoal briquets to the coals. Let the fresh briquets burn until they are almost completely covered with white ash. Spread the coals in an even layer and return the grill grate.

5. Return the ribs to the grill. Brush with half of the sauce, turn the ribs, and brush with the remaining sauce. Grill until the undersides are glazed, about 2 minutes. Turn and glaze the other sides about 2 minutes longer. Transfer to a cutting board. Let stand for 5 minutes, cut into individual ribs, and serve hot.

THE EASIEST BBQ RIBS

In an attempt to speed up the cooking, too many grill cooks fall back on precooking the ribs by boiling or baking them before putting them on the grill. In either case, this leaves lots of flavor behind. If you want **tender ribs in less time** than the traditional long-smoked barbecue, try this method. Foil-wrapped ribs are grilled over coals, where they cook until tender in their own juices, and are then subsequently sauced. They won't be smoky, but they will be **succulent, spicy, and delicious.**

5 POUNDS SPARERIBS, CUT INTO 3 SLABS

1¾ TEASPOONS SALT

⅓ CUP THE ULTIMATE SPICE RUB (PAGE 34)

BIG APPLE BARBECUE SAUCE (PAGE 18) OR YANKEE MAPLE BARBECUE SAUCE (PAGE 18)

1. Season the ribs all over with the salt, then sprinkle with the spice rub. Wrap each slab in a double thickness of heavy-duty aluminum foil. Let stand while building the fire.

2. Build a charcoal fire in an outdoor grill for direct high grilling (page 8) and let burn until the coals are almost completely covered with white ash.

3. Spread out the coals and replace the grill grate. Place the foil-wrapped ribs on the grill and cover. Adjust the vents to partially open to maintain the heat to medium. Grill, occasionally turning the packets with long tongs without piercing the foil, for 45 minutes. Open the vents all the way. Cover and grill, occasionally turning the packets, until the ribs are tender (open a packet to check, but be careful, as the juices are hot and steamy), about 30 minutes more. Transfer the packets to a platter. Open carefully and discard the juices.

4. Remove the grill grate from the grill and add about 3 pounds of charcoal briquets to the coals. Let the fresh briquets burn until they are almost completely covered with white ash. Spread the coals in an even layer and return the grate to the grill.

5. Return the ribs to the grill. Brush with half of the sauce, turn the ribs, and brush with the remaining sauce. Grill until the undersides are glazed, about 2 minutes. Turn and glaze the other sides about 2 minutes longer. Transfer to a cutting board. Let stand for 5 minutes, cut into individual ribs, and serve hot.

CHAPEL HILL CHOPPED PORK BARBECUE

MAKES 8 TO 10 SERVINGS
Grilling Method: Indirect Low

In North Carolina, nuances of barbecued pork shoulder seem to change from town to town. At least around Raleigh and Chapel Hill, there are a few constants, including hickory smoke, a **peppery thin sauce,** and a side of coleslaw.

PORK SHOULDER

2 TEASPOONS SWEET PAPRIKA, PREFERABLY HUNGARIAN OR SPANISH

2 TEASPOONS DRIED SAGE

1 TEASPOON FENNEL SEEDS, GROUND IN A MORTAR OR SPICE GRINDER (OPTIONAL)

1 TEASPOON ONION POWDER

1 TEASPOON GARLIC POWDER

1 TEASPOON SALT

1/2 TEASPOON FRESHLY GROUND BLACK PEPPER

1/4 TEASPOON CAYENNE PEPPER

ONE 71/2-POUND PORK SHOULDER WITH SKIN AND BONE

6 OR 7 HANDFULS HICKORY WOOD CHIPS, SOAKED FOR AT LEAST 30 MINUTES IN COLD WATER TO COVER

TWO 12-OUNCE BOTTLES HARD CIDER

HOT-SWEET SAUCE

11/4 CUPS CIDER VINEGAR

1/4 CUP SUGAR

1 TABLESPOON CRUSHED HOT RED PEPPER

2 GARLIC CLOVES, CRUSHED THROUGH A PRESS

1/2 TEASPOON SALT

SLAW

1 POUND COLESLAW MIX

1/3 CUP PLUS 1 TABLESPOON VEGETABLE OIL

3 TABLESPOONS HOT-SWEET SAUCE

SALT AND FRESHLY GROUND BLACK PEPPER TO TASTE

12 SOFT HAMBURGER ROLLS, FOR SERVING

1. Mix together the paprika, sage, fennel, if using, onion and garlic powders, salt, pepper, and cayenne in a small bowl. Using a sharp knife, trim away the skin from the pork shoulder, leaving a 2-inch-wide band of skin around the shank. Trim off most of the fat, leaving a 1/4-inch-thick layer. Sprinkle the rub all over the pork, cover, and let stand at room temperature while building the fire.

2. Build a charcoal fire in an outdoor grill for indirect low grilling (page 9) and let burn until the coals are almost completely covered with white ash.

3. Add 1 cup water to a drip pan. Add a handful of drained chips to the coals. Lightly oil the grill grate. Place the pork over the drip pan and cover the grill. Grill until the pork is very tender and an instant-read thermometer inserted in the center of the pork reads 190°F, 5 to 6 hours. During this period, adjust the vents as needed to keep the temperature around 325°F, because long, slow cooking will melt the fat and gristle to make the meat especially juicy and tender. After 45 minutes, and every 45 minutes or so after that, add 10 briquets and a handful of drained chips to maintain the temperature. When you add the briquets, baste the pork with the cider. When the pork is done, the exterior will be very dark, almost black. Transfer the pork to a carving board and let stand for 20 to 30 minutes.

4. Meanwhile, to make the hot-sweet sauce, whisk the vinegar, sugar, red pepper, garlic, and salt in a bowl to dissolve the sugar. Pour the sauce into a pitcher and set aside.

5. To make the slaw, mix together the cole slaw mix, oil, and hot-sweet sauce in a large bowl. Season with salt and pepper. Cover and refrigerate until ready to serve.

6. To serve, carve the meat—it should be so tender that it is almost falls from the bone. Using a large knife, coarsely chop the meat and transfer to a large bowl. Season the meat with about ½ cup of the hot-sweet sauce. Serve with the slaw, rolls, and remaining sauce.

MEMPHIS-STYLE BABY BACK RIBS

MAKES 6 SERVINGS

Grilling Method: Indirect Low

In most barbecue places in Tennessee, you will be hard pressed to find ribs that have been sauced—it's all about the **smoke and the spice.** Baby back ribs may have less meat on them than spareribs, but that meat is **tender and flavorful.** And it cooks in less time than their chunkier cousins. If you want to use spareribs, allow about 2½ hours.

6 POUNDS BABY RACK RIBS, CUT INTO 3 OR 4 SLABS

2 TEASPOONS SALT

⅓ CUP THE ULTIMATE SPICE RUB (PAGE 34)

2 HANDFULS HICKORY WOOD CHIPS, SOAKED IN WATER TO COVER FOR AT LEAST 30 MINUTES, DRAINED

1. Season the ribs all over with the salt, then sprinkle with the spice rub. Cover and let stand while building the fire.

2. Build a charcoal fire in an outdoor grill for indirect low grilling (page 9) and let burn until the coals are almost completely covered with white ash.

3. Lightly oil the grill grate. Sprinkle a handful of chips over the coals. Add 2 cups water to a drip pan. Place the ribs over the drip pan and cover. Grill for 45 minutes. Toss the remaining chips on the coals, add 6 briquets to the coals to maintain the temperature, and turn the ribs. Continue grilling until the ribs are fork-tender, about 1¾ hours longer.

4. Transfer the ribs to a carving board and let stand for 5 minutes. Chop between the bones and serve hot.

SAUSAGES WITH SWEET PEPPERS AND ONIONS

MAKES 4 TO 6 SERVINGS
Grilling Method: Banked

Usually you'll find sausage and peppers served up from a skillet, but the grill does a terrific job with this dish, too. Grilled over coals, the sausages acquire more flavor from the increased browning. Wrapped in a foil packet, the vegetables cook in their own juices and are especially **sweet and tender.**

1 LARGE ONION, CUT INTO ¼-INCH-THICK HALF-MOONS

2 RED BELL PEPPERS, SEEDED AND RIBBED, CUT INTO ¼-INCH-WIDE STRIPS ABOUT 2 INCHES LONG

6 GARLIC CLOVES, SLICED

2 TABLESPOONS EXTRA-VIRGIN OLIVE OIL

1 TEASPOON DRIED OREGANO

SALT AND FRESHLY GROUND PEPPER TO TASTE

6 PORK OR TURKEY ITALIAN SAUSAGES, EACH PIERCED IN A FEW PLACES WITH A FORK

1. Build a charcoal fire in an outdoor grill for banked grilling (page 10) and let burn until the coals are almost completely covered with white ash.

2. Meanwhile, tear off a 24-inch length of heavy-duty aluminum foil and place on a work surface. Toss the onions, bell peppers, garlic, oil, and oregano in a large bowl and season with the salt and pepper. Heap the vegetables on the foil, fold the foil over to enclose them, and crimp the open sides to make a packet.

3. Place the packet of vegetables over the hotter area of the grill and cover. Grill for 5 minutes. Move the packet to the cooler area of the grill. Place the sausages on the hotter area, cover, and grill, turning occasionally, until browned on all sides, about 6 minutes. Move to the cooler area with the vegetable packet, cover, and grill until the sausages show no sign of pink in the center when pierced with the tip of a knife and the vegetables are tender, about 5 minutes longer. Open the vegetable packet and serve with the sausages.

GRILLED HOT DOGS WITH HOMEMADE CUCUMBER RELISH

MAKES 12 SERVINGS
Grilling Method: Banked

How to make **hot dogs cool?** Make your own relish. It is surprisingly simple, and remains fresh and crisp, unlike the bottled version. Search out the best franks in town to share the plate with your **homemade relish.**

RELISH

3 TABLESPOONS DISTILLED WHITE VINEGAR

1 TABLESPOON SUGAR

1 1/2 TEASPOONS YELLOW MUSTARD SEEDS

2 KIRBY CUCUMBERS, SCRUBBED, HALVED LENGTHWISE, SEEDS REMOVED, AND CUT INTO 1/4- TO 1/2-INCH DICE

3/4 TEASPOON SALT

1 TABLESPOON VEGETABLE OIL

3/4 CUP 1/4- TO 1/2-INCH-DICE RED BELL PEPPER

3/4 CUP FINELY CHOPPED ONION

12 HOT DOGS, EACH PIERCED IN A FEW PLACES WITH A FORK

12 HOT DOG BUNS

MUSTARD AND TOMATO KETCHUP, FOR SERVING

1. To make the relish, combine the vinegar, sugar, and mustard seeds in a small bowl. Toss the cucumbers and salt in a colander. Let the vinegar mixture and cucumbers stand separate for 1 hour. Rinse the cucumbers under cold water, drain and pat dry with paper towels. Transfer the cucumbers to a small bowl.

2. Heat the oil in a medium skillet over medium heat. Add the red pepper and onion and cook, stirring occasionally, until crisp-tender, about 3 minutes. Stir into the cucumbers. Add the vinegar mixture and mix well. Cover and refrigerate, to blend the flavors, for at least 4 hours. (The relish can be made up to 2 days ahead, covered and refrigerated.) Remove from the refrigerator 1 hour before serving.

3. Build a charcoal fire in an outdoor grill for banked grilling (page 10) and let burn until the coals are almost completely covered with white ash.

4. Lightly oil the grill grate. Place the hot dogs over the hotter area of the grill and cover. Grill, turning occasionally, until seared with grill marks, about 2 minutes. Move to the cooler area and grill until the hot dogs are heated through, about 5 minutes longer. During the last few minutes, place the hot dog buns on the grill to toast and heat through. Serve hot, with the buns, relish, mustard, and ketchup.

GLAZED PORK BURGERS WITH PICKLED BEAN SPROUTS

MAKES 4 SERVINGS
Grilling Method: Banked

When building skills as a grill cook, it's important to master old favorites like hamburgers, but it is equally important to expand your repertoire. Pork burgers glossed with a rich **teriyaki-like glaze** and topped with crunchy, **quickly pickled bean sprouts** (no canning required) are sure to spark a conversation around the picnic table, and to have folks asking for seconds, too.

PICKLED BEAN SPROUTS

1/2 CUP UNSEASONED RICE VINEGAR

1 SCALLION, WHITE AND GREEN PARTS, CUT IN HALF

ONE 1-INCH LENGTH FRESH GINGER, SLICED (NO NEED TO PEEL)

1 GARLIC CLOVE, CRUSHED UNDER A KNIFE AND PEELED

1 TABLESPOON PLAIN TABLE SALT (IF USING KOSHER OR SEA SALT, USE A HEAPING TABLESPOON)

12 OUNCES FRESH BEAN SPROUTS

1 TABLESPOON ASIAN DARK SESAME OIL

GLAZED PORK

2 TABLESPOONS MOLASSES

2 TABLESPOONS SOY SAUCE

1 TEASPOON GROUND GINGER

1/2 TEASPOON GARLIC POWDER

1/2 TEASPOON ONION POWDER

1 1/2 POUNDS GROUND PORK

2 TABLESPOONS DRIED UNFLAVORED BREAD CRUMBS

1 TEASPOON SALT

1/2 TEASPOON FRESHLY GROUND PEPPER

4 HAMBURGER BUNS

1. To make the bean sprouts, bring the vinegar, scallion, ginger, garlic, salt, and 1 quart water to a boil in a large saucepan over high heat. Place the bean sprouts in a heatproof medium bowl and add the vinegar mixture. Let stand at room temperature for 1 hour. Drain in a colander, removing the scallion, ginger, and garlic. Transfer to a bowl and stir in the sesame oil. Let stand at room temperature until ready to serve. (The bean sprouts can be made up to 8 hours ahead. They are best the day they are made.)

2. To make the glazed pork, whisk together the molasses, soy sauce, ginger, garlic powder, and onion powder in a small bowl.

3. Mix the pork, bread crumbs, salt, pepper, and 2 tablespoons of glaze in a medium bowl until combined. Reserve the remaining glaze. Form into four 4-inch patties. Place on a waxed paper–lined plate, cover, and let stand at room temperature while building the fire. (The burgers can be made up to 8 hours ahead, covered, and refrigerated. Remove from the refrigerator 30 minutes before grilling.)

4. Build a charcoal fire in an outdoor grill for banked grilling (page 10) and let burn until the coals are almost completely covered with white ash.

5. Lightly oil the grill grate. Place the burgers over the hotter area of the grill and cover. Cook until the underside is browned, about 3 minutes. Turn and brown the other side. Transfer to the cooler area of the grill and cover. Cook, turning occasionally, until the burgers feel firm and spring back when pressed in the centers, about 6 minutes more. If using an instant-read thermometer, insert it horizontally through the side of the burger to reach the center—it should read 150°F. During the last few minutes, brush the tops of the burgers with the remaining glaze, and place the buns on the grill to warm and toast.

6. Place a burger on each bun, top with a handful of pickled sprouts, and serve hot, with the remaining sprouts passed on the side.

POULTRY

RUBBED, SAUCED, AND SMOKED GRILLED CHICKEN

CLASSIC

MAKES 6 TO 8 SERVINGS
Grilling Method: Indirect High

Chicken pieces cooking on a backyard grill, slathered with **sweet-tangy sauce,** is an image that sums up charcoal grilling in a savory nutshell. This variation of the indirect method gives **perfectly cooked, juicy results.** The combination of spices, sauce, and smoke elevates this familiar fare to a new level. There are many ways to personalize chicken, so use this method as your jumping-off place.

TWO 4-POUND CHICKENS, EACH CUT INTO 2 DRUMSTICKS, 2 THIGHS, 2 BREAST HALVES, AND 2 WINGS

SALT TO TASTE

3 TABLESPOONS THE ULTIMATE SPICE RUB (PAGE 34)

1 HANDFUL HICKORY OR MESQUITE WOOD CHIPS, SOAKED IN WATER FOR AT LEAST 30 MINUTES, DRAINED

1½ CUPS ALL-AMERICAN BARBECUE SAUCE (PAGE 18), OR USE YOUR FAVORITE HOMEMADE OR STORE-BOUGHT SAUCE

1. Build a charcoal fire in an outdoor grill for indirect high grilling (see page 10) and let burn until the coals are almost completely covered with white ash. Leave the coals heaped in the center of the grill and do not spread them out. (If using a chimney starter, dump the coals in the center of the grill.)

2. Season the chicken pieces with the salt and then sprinkle with the rub.

3. Toss the drained chips on the coals. Lightly oil the grill grate. Place the chicken, skin side down, on the outside perimeter of the grill, around, but not over, the coals. Cover and grill for 15 minutes. Turn the chicken and continue grilling until an instant-read thermometer inserted in the thickest part of a breast without touching a bone reads 170°F, about 20 minutes more. A few minutes before the chicken is done, brush the top of it with half of the barbecue sauce.

4. Turn the chicken and brush with the remaining barbecue sauce. Move the chicken, with the freshly sauced side down, directly over the coals until the undersides are glazed, about 1 minute. Transfer the chicken to a platter and serve immediately.

TIPS FOR GRILLED CHICKEN

- Most of us were taught to grill chicken directly over the coals. However, the fat in the chicken skin renders directly onto the coals, making flare-ups inevitable. This indirect method gives crisp skin without the grill cook becoming a firefighter.

- Overcooked chicken is dry and tough. Cook the chicken just until an instant-read thermometer registers 170°F in a breast piece, or the chicken shows no sign of pink when pierced at the bone of a thigh piece.

- Other rub or herb paste options include Tex-Mex Rub (page 36), Mediterranean Herb Paste (page 39), or Indian Spice Rub (page 38). Chile fans will love the Tex-Mex Rub slathered with Orange-Chipotle Barbecue Sauce (page 22).

MAPLE AND ROSEMARY BRINED CHICKEN

MAKES 6 TO 8 SERVINGS

Grilling Method: Indirect Medium

The brine for this moist and tender bird has **a touch of sweetness from maple,** as well as rosemary's fragrance. We use a large roasting chicken here because even if you don't need a lot of servings for the meal at hand, it could provide leftovers for sandwiches, salads, and other dishes.

MAPLE-ROSEMARY BRINE

2 QUARTS ICE WATER

⅔ CUP PURE MAPLE SYRUP, PREFERABLY GRADE B (SEE NOTE), OR MAPLE-FLAVORED PANCAKE SYRUP

½ CUP SALT

3 TABLESPOONS CHOPPED FRESH ROSEMARY, OR 2 TABLESPOONS DRIED ROSEMARY

1 TEASPOON MAPLE EXTRACT (OPTIONAL, IF USING PURE MAPLE SYRUP)

ONE 7½-POUND ROASTING CHICKEN

3 HANDFULS MAPLE OR HICKORY CHIPS, SOAKED IN COLD WATER TO COVER FOR AT LEAST 30 MINUTES THEN DRAINED

1. To make the brine, stir the ice water, syrup, salt, rosemary, and maple extract, if using, together in a large nonreactive (stainless-steel or enameled cast-iron) pot to dissolve the salt. (A tall 6-quart plastic food storage container works well for this, too.)

2. Remove the pads of yellow fat from the tail area of the chicken. Add the chicken to the brine. Refrigerate for at least 6 and up to 10 hours, no longer.

3. Build a charcoal fire in an outdoor grill for indirect medium grilling (see page 9) and let burn until the coals are almost completely covered with white ash.

4. Drain the chicken and discard the brine. Pat the chicken dry with paper towels. Toss a handful of chips on the coals. Add 1 cup water to a drip pan. Place the chicken over the drip pan. Adjust the vents so the temperature averages 350°F. Cover and grill for 1 hour. Add another handful of chips and 12 briquets to the coals. Cover and grill for 1 hour more. Add the remaining chips to the coals, and a few more briquets, if needed to maintain the 350°F temperature. Cover again and grill until a meat thermometer inserted in the thickest part of the thigh not touching a bone reads 170°F, about 30 minutes longer.

5. Transfer the chicken to a carving board. Let stand 15 minutes, then carve the chicken. Do not be surprised to see pink meat just under the skin—this is where the smoke entered the chicken, and is not undercooked meat. Serve hot.

Note: Pure maple syrup is gently flavored. Commercial pancake syrup has a stronger maple taste, thanks to artificial flavorings. There are two grades of pure maple syrup. Grade A is quite subtle, and perhaps best for pouring over breakfast treats from the griddle, where its flavor can shine. Grade B is more robust, and preferable for using as a cooking ingredient. In either case, when using pure maple syrup, you can increase the maple flavor with the addition of maple extract, either natural or imitation.

CAESAR CHICKEN WITH ROMAINE HEARTS

MAKES 4 SERVINGS
Grilling Method: Banked

Caesar salad used to be a somewhat snooty dish that you could get only at a "fancy" restaurant. While the salad was originally a vegetable salad (some say it was actually romaine leaves and a thick dip, not a salad), when people discovered that it could be bolstered with chicken breast, there was **no stopping its popularity.** The chicken-and-lettuce combination is now a staple in homes and eateries all over the country. The following recipe uses the same mixture as a marinade and as the salad dressing, marrying the flavors of different components.

CAESAR DRESSING

1½ CUPS MAYONNAISE

3 TABLESPOONS FRESH LEMON JUICE

1½ TEASPOONS ANCHOVY PASTE
(SEE NOTE)

3 GARLIC CLOVES, CRUSHED THROUGH A
GARLIC PRESS

¾ TEASPOON FRESHLY GROUND BLACK
PEPPER

FOUR 7-OUNCE BONELESS AND SKINLESS
CHICKEN BREAST HALVES

2 ROMAINE LETTUCE HEARTS, TORN INTO
BITE-SIZED PIECES

⅓ CUP FRESHLY GRATED ROMANO OR
PARMESAN CHEESE

1. To make the dressing, whisk the mayonnaise, lemon juice, anchovy paste, garlic, and pepper in a medium bowl until combined. Transfer ¾ cup of the dressing to a resealable plastic bag. Add the chicken, close the bag, and turn to coat the chicken in the marinade. Refrigerate for at least 1 and up to 8 hours. Remove from the refrigerator 30 minutes before grilling. Cover and refrigerate the remaining dressing.

2. Build a charcoal fire in an outdoor grill for banked grilling (see page 10), and let burn until the coals are almost completely covered with white ash.

3. Lightly oil the grill grate. Remove the chicken from the marinade. Place the chicken on the cooler side of the grill and cover. Cook until the underside is browned, about 6 minutes. Turn and cook until the chicken feels firm when pressed, about 6 minutes more. Transfer the chicken to a cutting board and let stand about 3 minutes. Holding the knife at a slight diagonal, cut each breast into ½-inch-thick slices.

4. Toss the romaine with the reserved dressing. Divide the salad among 4 dinner plates and sprinkle with the cheese. Top with equal amounts of the sliced chicken and serve immediately.

Note: Anchovy paste is a secret ingredient to Caesar salad dressing—don't leave it out! While you can use canned anchovy fillets and mince them, anchovy paste in a tube is much more convenient. You'll find it in the canned fish department of supermarkets and Italian delicatessens.

TERIYAKI CHICKEN BREASTS WITH ASIAN NOODLE SALAD

MAKES 4 SERVINGS
Grilling Method: Banked

Here, Asian-inspired **teriyaki sauce does double duty** as a chicken marinade and a dressing for a satisfying noodle salad. Make the marinade first and reserve ⅓ cup for the salad—marinades that have touched raw meat should never be used for other purposes. While the vegetables are well suited to the salad, consider asparagus, celery, or carrots, too.

FOUR 7-OUNCE BONELESS AND SKINLESS CHICKEN BREAST HALVES, LIGHTLY POUNDED TO EQUAL THICKNESS

⅔ CUP TERIYAKI MARINADE (PAGE 30)

ASIAN NOODLE SALAD

1 CUP (4 OUNCES) SUGAR SNAP PEAS

8 OUNCES DRIED LINGUINE

1 MEDIUM CUCUMBER, PEELED, HALVED LENGTHWISE, SEEDS REMOVED, CUT INTO THIN HALF-MOONS

1 SMALL RED PEPPER, SEEDS AND RIBS DISCARDED, CUT INTO THIN STRIPS

2 SCALLIONS, WHITE AND GREEN PARTS, THINLY SLICED

⅓ CUP TERIYAKI MARINADE, STRAINED

1 TABLESPOON UNSEASONED RICE VINEGAR

2 TEASPOONS SESAME SEEDS, TOASTED (SEE NOTE)

1. Place the chicken in a self-sealing bag and add ⅔ cup of the marinade. Refrigerate, turning occasionally, for at least 1 and up to 8 hours. Remove from the refrigerator 30 minutes before grilling.

2. To make the noodle salad, bring a large pot of lightly salted water to a boil over high heat. Add the sugar snap peas and cook until they are crisp-tender, about 2 minutes. Scoop them from the water with a wire sieve, rinse under cold water, and set aside.

3. Add the linguine to the water and cook until tender, according to the package directions. Drain in a colander, rinse under cold water, and drain again well. Transfer to a large bowl. Add the sugar snap peas, cucumber, red pepper, scallions, strained marinade, and vinegar and mix well. Cover and refrigerate until ready to serve.

4. Build a charcoal fire in an outdoor grill for banked grilling (see page 10), and let burn until the coals are almost completely covered with white ash.

5. Lightly oil the grill grate. Remove the chicken from the marinade. Place the chicken on the cooler area of the grill and cover. Cook, turning once, until the chicken feels firm when pressed, 10 to 12 minutes. Transfer the chicken to a cutting board and let stand about 3 minutes. Holding the knife at a slight diagonal, cut each breast into ½-inch-thick slices.

6. Divide the noodle salad among 4 dinner plates. Place a chicken breast, fanning out the slices, next to each salad, and sprinkle with the sesame seeds. Serve immediately.

Note: To toast sesame seeds, heat an empty skillet over medium heat. Add the seeds and cook, stirring often, until the seeds are fragrant and lightly toasted, about 1 minute. Immediately pour the seeds onto a plate and cool.

CHICKEN BREASTS WITH WILD MUSHROOM STUFFING

MAKES 4 SERVINGS
Grilling Method: Indirect High

Boneless and skinless chicken breast may be fast and easy to cook, but this recipe is the perfect example of why one should not overlook breasts on the bone. By slipping an **earthy mushroom stuffing** under the skin and grilling the breast on the bone, you'll get extra flavor and juiciness in every bite. The **indulgent cream sauce** is tasty as anything you'll get at a fine French restaurant, but also very easy.

WILD MUSHROOM STUFFING

10 OUNCES CREMINI MUSHROOMS (BABY PORTOBELLOS)

1 TABLESPOON OLIVE OIL

1 TABLESPOON FINELY CHOPPED SHALLOTS

1 GARLIC CLOVE, MINCED

1 CUP FRESH BREAD CRUMBS

1½ TEASPOONS DRIED PORCINI POWDER (OPTIONAL, SEE NOTE)

1 TEASPOON CHOPPED FRESH THYME, OR ½ TEASPOON DRIED THYME

SALT AND FRESHLY GROUND BLACK PEPPER TO TASTE

FOUR 11-OUNCE CHICKEN BREAST HALVES WITH SKIN AND BONE

SALT AND FRESHLY GROUND BLACK PEPPER TO TASTE

THYME CREAM SAUCE

1 CUP CHICKEN BROTH, PREFERABLY HOMEMADE, OR USE REDUCED-SODIUM CANNED BROTH

1¼ CUPS HEAVY CREAM

½ TEASPOON CHOPPED FRESH THYME, OR ¼ TEASPOON DRIED THYME

SALT AND FRESHLY GROUND BLACK PEPPER TO TASTE

1. Build a charcoal fire in an outdoor grill for indirect high grilling (see page 10) and let burn until the coals are almost completely covered with white ash.

2. Wash the mushrooms well under cold running water. Coarsely chop them—they can be chunky. In batches, pulse the mushrooms in a food processor until they are finely chopped. (You can also use a large knife to chop them.) Transfer the mushrooms to a bowl.

3. Heat the oil in a large skillet over medium-high heat. Add the chopped mushrooms and cook uncovered, stirring often, until they give off their juices, about 4 minutes. Add the shallots and garlic and cook, stirring often, until the mushrooms are quite dry and beginning to brown, about 4 minutes more. Remove from the heat and stir in the bread crumbs, mushroom powder (if using), and thyme. Season with salt and pepper.

4. Starting at the meaty side of each breast, slip your fingers under the skin and loosen it, keeping the skin attached at the opposite side. Spoon equal amounts of the stuffing under the skin. Smooth the stuffing under the skin to distribute it evenly. Season the chicken with salt and pepper.

5. Lightly oil the grill grate. Place the chicken, skin side up, over a drip pan. Add 1 cup water to the drip pan. Cover and grill until an instant-read thermometer inserted in the thickest part of the breast without touching a bone reads 170°F, about 35 minutes.

6. Meanwhile, make the sauce. Bring the broth to a boil in a medium saucepan over high heat. Cook until the broth reduces to about 2 tablespoons, about 12 minutes. Add the cream and thyme. Return to the boil, taking care that the cream does not boil over. Cook, stirring occasionally, until the sauce thickens and reduces to about ⅔ cup, about 10 minutes. Season with salt and pepper. Keep the sauce warm.

7. Serve the chicken hot with a spoonful of the sauce over each breast.

Note: Dried porcini powder has an advantage over sliced dried mushrooms. The latter needs to be soaked in hot water before using, and because the soaking water contains flavor leached from the mushrooms, the cook has to utilize the liquid. A sprinkle of powder gives a boost of porcini flavor without the hassle of soaking. It is available at specialty food stores, but it is easy to make your own. Simply grind about ½ cup loosely packed dried porcini mushrooms into a fine powder in an electric spice grinder (a coffee grinder reserved for spices) or a blender.

BUFFALO CHICKEN SANDWICHES

MAKES 4 SANDWICHES
Grilling Method: Banked

If you deconstructed Buffalo chicken wings, then put the chicken, hot sauce, butter, blue cheese dressing, and celery back together, you might end up with these equally tasty Buffalo chicken sandwiches. Vary the spiciness with **your favorite hot pepper sauce,** from traditional red sauce, habañero and jalapeño sauces, and beyond.

BLUE CHEESE AND CELERY MAYONNAISE

⅓ CUP MAYONNAISE

1 MEDIUM CELERY RIB, FINELY CHOPPED

1½ OUNCES BLUE CHEESE, CRUMBLED (⅓ CUP)

FRESHLY GROUND BLACK PEPPER TO TASTE

FOUR 6-OUNCE BONELESS AND SKINLESS CHICKEN BREAST HALVES

3 TABLESPOONS UNSALTED BUTTER

2 TEASPOONS HOT PEPPER SAUCE

SALT TO TASTE

4 KAISER ROLLS, SPLIT IN HALF

SLICED TOMATOES AND LETTUCE, FOR SERVING

1. To make the blue cheese mayonnaise, use a rubber spatula to mix the mayonnaise, celery, and blue cheese together in a small bowl, mashing some of the blue cheese as you mix. Season with the pepper. Set aside while grilling the chicken breasts.

2. Build a charcoal fire in an outdoor grill for banked grilling (see page 10) and let burn until the coals are almost completely covered with white ash.

3. Lightly pound the chicken breasts with a flat meat pounder to an even thickness. Place the breasts on a plate. Melt the butter in a saucepan over low heat or in a microwave. Add the hot pepper sauce. Pour half of the butter mixture over the breasts, and turn the breasts to coat them on both sides. Season the breasts with salt.

4. Lightly oil the grill plate. Place the chicken on the cooler side of the grill and cover. Cook until the underside is browned, about 6 minutes. Turn and cook until the chicken feels firm when pressed, about 6 minutes more, basting occasionally with the remaining butter mixture. During the last minute or so, place the rolls, cut sides down, over the hotter side of the grill to toast.

5. Spread each roll with the blue cheese mayonnaise. Top each of the bottom halves of the rolls with a chicken breast, sliced tomatoes, and lettuce. Cover with the top halves and serve.

MOROCCAN CHICKEN KEBABS WITH CARROT-SCALLION SALAD

MAKES 4 SERVINGS
Grilling Method: Banked

For **reliably succulent** chicken kebabs, choose chicken thighs, which cook up moist and juicy. Grilling the kebabs over moderate, not high, heat, allows both the chicken and vegetables to cook at the same rate. As added insurance against overcooked vegetables, cut them on the large side. This is **a light and satisfying meal,** but for a starchy side dish, you may serve couscous to keep in the Moroccan spirit.

CARROT-SCALLION SALAD

2 TABLESPOONS CHERMOULA (PAGE 40)

1 TABLESPOON FRESH LEMON JUICE

3 TABLESPOONS EXTRA-VIRGIN OLIVE OIL

5 LARGE CARROTS (12 OUNCES), SCRUBBED BUT NOT PEELED, SHREDDED IN A FOOD PROCESSOR OR WITH A BOX GRATER

1 LARGE SCALLION, WHITE AND GREEN PARTS, TRIMMED AND FINELY CHOPPED

SALT AND FRESHLY GROUND BLACK PEPPER TO TASTE

KEBABS

4 BONELESS AND SKINLESS CHICKEN THIGHS, EACH CUT INTO 4 PIECES

½ CUP CHERMOULA (PAGE 40)

1 LARGE ZUCCHINI, TRIMMED AND SLICED CROSSWISE INTO 8 ROUNDS ABOUT 1 INCH THICK

½ LARGE RED BELL PEPPER, SEEDS AND RIBS REMOVED, CUT INTO 8 PIECES ABOUT 1 INCH SQUARE

1 TABLESPOON EXTRA-VIRGIN OLIVE OIL

SALT AND FRESHLY GROUND BLACK PEPPER TO TASTE

1. To make the carrot slaw, mix the chermoula, lemon juice, and olive oil together in a medium bowl. Add the carrots and scallion and mix again. Season with salt and pepper.

Cover and refrigerate until ready to serve. (The salad can be made up to 8 hours ahead, covered, and refrigerated.)

2. For the kebabs, combine the chicken and chermoula in a resealable plastic bag. Refrigerate for at least 1 and up to 8 hours. Remove the chicken from the refrigerator 30 minutes before grilling.

3. Build a charcoal fire in an outdoor grill for banked grilling (see page 10) and let burn until the coals are almost completely covered with white ash.

4. Toss the zucchini and red pepper with the olive oil in a medium bowl and season with the salt and pepper. On each of 4 metal skewers, thread 4 chicken pieces, 2 zucchini pieces, and 2 red pepper pieces, alternating the chicken with the vegetables. Do not crowd the ingredients on the skewer. Discard the chermoula in the plastic bag.

5. Lightly oil the grilling grate. Place the kebabs over the cooler side of the grill and cover. Cook, turning occasionally, until the chicken feels firm when pressed and shows no sign of pink when pierced with a small sharp knife, 16 to 18 minutes.

6. Spoon equal amounts of the salad onto 4 dinner plates. Slide the chicken and vegetables from each skewer onto each plate. Serve hot.

APPLE CIDER-BRINED GRILLED TURKEY

MAKES 12 SERVINGS
Grilling Method: Indirect Medium

Make turkey on the grill and you may never roast one in the oven again. Brining guarantees a moist bird, but it is difficult to make room in a refrigerator to hold the bird and brine. Instead, contain the bagged and brined bird in larger roasting pans and keep chilled in an ice chest. The pan drippings will be too salty (and perhaps too smoky) to use for gravy—a gravy that is made ahead without drippings solves that dilemma. One more tip, concerning weather: Because cold November weather can affect the grill temperature, complicating the timing, simply grill the turkey to get smoke and charcoal flavor, then roast until done. If you want to continue cooking the bird outside, go ahead.

APPLE CIDER BRINE (PAGE 42)

ONE 12-POUND FRESH TURKEY, GIBLETS RESERVED

1 LARGE ONION, CHOPPED

1 GRANNY SMITH APPLE, CORED AND CHOPPED

4 HANDFULS OF APPLE OR OTHER FRUIT WOOD CHIPS SOAKED FOR AT LEAST 30 MINUTES THEN DRAIN

HEAD-START GRAVY (PAGE 168)

1. The night before, make the brine. Place the turkey in 2 turkey-size roasting bags in an ice chest. Add the brine, press out excess air from the bag, and secure the bag with a rubber band. Add ice packs or ice cubes to the chest and close. Chill the turkey for at least 8 and up to 12 hours.

2. Build a charcoal fire in an outdoor grill for indirect medium grilling (see page 9) and let burn until the coals are almost completely covered with white ash. You will not need a drip pan.

3. Remove the turkey from the brine, rinse under cold water, and pat dry with paper towels. Mix the onion and apple together in a bowl. Tuck the wings akimbo, tucking the tips behind the turkey's shoulders. Stuff the neck cavity with some of the apple mixture, and pin the neck skin to the back skin with a small wooden or metal skewer. Stuff the remaining mixture into the body cavity. (The apple mixture is merely a seasoning, and keeps the neck area from looking sunken. Do not serve it.) Place the drumsticks in the plastic or wire holder at the turkey tail, or tie them together with kitchen string. Insert one heavy-duty disposable aluminum foil roasting pan inside a second pan. Place a roasting rack in the doubled pan, and then the turkey on the rack.

4. Place the turkey in the pans on the grill grate over the empty area of the grill. Pour 1 cup of water into the doubled roasting pans. Add a handful of chips to the coals and cover. Grill for 1 hour. Add the remaining chips and 10 briquets to the coals, cover, and grill for another hour.

5. Meanwhile, position a rack in the center of the oven and preheat to 350°F. Supporting the bottom of the pan, carefully transfer the turkey in the doubled pan to the oven. Roast, basting occasionally with the pan juices, until an instant-read thermometer inserted into meaty part of thigh, not touching the bone, registers 180°F, about 1 hour. Transfer the turkey to a platter and let stand for 20 minutes before carving. Carve the turkey and serve with the gravy.

HEAD-START GRAVY

If you have ever been caught in a bind when it comes to making gravy, this make-ahead version will come to your rescue. The gravy begins with a stock made from the turkey giblets—do not use the liver, which is too bitter when simmered for a long time.

2 TEASPOONS VEGETABLE OIL

NECK AND GIBLETS (NO LIVER) FROM 12-POUND TURKEY

1 MEDIUM ONION, CHOPPED

1 MEDIUM CARROT, CHOPPED

1 MEDIUM CELERY STALK, CHOPPED

1 QUART REDUCED-SODIUM CANNED CHICKEN BROTH

½ TEASPOON DRIED THYME

¼ TEASPOON WHOLE BLACK PEPPERCORNS

4 PARSLEY SPRIGS

1 BAY LEAF

4 TABLESPOONS (½ STICK) UNSALTED BUTTER, SOFTENED

¼ CUP ALL-PURPOSE FLOUR

SALT AND FRESHLY GROUND BLACK PEPPER TO TASTE

1. Heat the oil in a large pot over medium-high heat. Add the neck and giblets and cook, turning them occasionally, until browned, about 10 minutes. Add the onion, carrot, and celery and cook, stirring occasionally, until the vegetables soften, about 5 minutes longer. Add 3 cups water and cook, stirring up the browned bits in the pot with a wooden spoon. Add the broth and bring to a boil, skimming off the foam that rises to the surface. Add the thyme, peppercorns, parsley, and bay leaf. Reduce the heat to low and simmer, uncovered, until the stock is full-flavored, 2 to 3 hours. Strain in a colander placed over a bowl. Let stand 5 minutes, then skim off any fat from the surface of the stock. You should have 6 cups stock; add water, if needed, or reserve any excess stock for another use.

2. Heat an empty large saucepan over high heat. Add 1 cup of stock and boil until the stock is reduced to a dark brown glaze, about 5 minutes. Add 1 cup of stock and repeat.

3. Reduce the heat to medium. Add the butter to the pot and melt. Add the flour and whisk until smooth. Whisk in the remaining 4 cups of stock and bring to a boil. Cook at a brisk simmer, whisking often, until the gravy is thick enough to coat a wooden spoon, about 10 minutes. Season with salt and pepper. Serve hot.

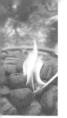

BEER-CAN CHICKEN

MAKES 4 SERVINGS
Grilling Method: Indirect High

Whoever conceived the grilling of a whole chicken **propped up on an open can of beer** should be inducted into the Grilling Hall of Fame. Don't be a skeptic about this procedure, for the steaming beer moistens the flesh from the **inside out,** while the spice-rubbed exterior skin gets crisp. There are all sorts of gadgets on the market for holding the chicken on the can, but an inexpensive metal pie plate works well, too.

ONE 4-POUND CHICKEN

1 TABLESPOON OLIVE OIL

SALT TO TASTE

1 TABLESPOON SWEET PAPRIKA, PREFERABLY SPANISH SMOKED

1 TEASPOON DRIED THYME

1 TEASPOON DRIED OREGANO

¼ TEASPOON GARLIC POWDER

⅛ TEASPOON CAYENNE PEPPER

ONE 12-OUNCE CAN LAGER BEER

1. Build a charcoal fire in an outdoor grill for indirect high grilling (see page 10) and let burn until the coals are almost completely covered with white ash. You will not need a drip pan.

2. Brush the chicken with the oil and season inside and out with the salt. Mix the paprika, thyme, oregano, garlic powder, and cayenne together in a small bowl. Sprinkle the spice mixture all over the outside of the chicken.

3. Place a disposable pie pan inside another identical pan. Open the beer can. Insert the beer can inside the body cavity of the chicken and stand the can with the chicken on the doubled pie plates, adjusting the chicken and can as needed so the chicken balances. Let stand at room temperature until the coals are ready.

4. Place the pie plates with the chicken and beer over the empty part of the grill. Cover and grill until the chicken is deeply browned and an instant-read thermometer inserted in the thickest part of the thigh, not touching a bone, reads 170°F, about 1 hour, 10 minutes.

5. Using pot holders and tongs, remove the chicken from the can. Take care, as some of the beer will have boiled over into the aluminum pan. Transfer the chicken to a carving board. Let stand 5 to 10 minutes, then chop into serving pieces. Serve hot.

TURKEY BREAST WITH THANKSGIVING HERB BUTTER

MAKES 8 SERVINGS
Grilling Method: Indirect High

For **smaller holiday gatherings,** consider grilling a turkey breast rather than a whole bird. It is stuffed under the skin with a butter flavored with the familiar herbs that find their way into almost every holiday turkey—parsley, sage, rosemary, thyme, and marjoram, which are now packaged together as "poultry seasoning." This is also a great recipe for weekend grilling, as it could supply turkey for **quite a few sandwiches** during the work week. Oak or grapevine chips go especially well with the herb flavors, but skip the chips if you prefer.

ONE 5½-POUND WHOLE TURKEY BREAST

6 TABLESPOONS UNSALTED BUTTER, AT ROOM TEMPERATURE

1 TABLESPOON CHOPPED FRESH PARSLEY

2 TEASPOONS CHOPPED FRESH SAGE

2 TEASPOONS CHOPPED FRESH ROSEMARY

2 TEASPOONS CHOPPED FRESH THYME

2 TEASPOONS CHOPPED FRESH MARJORAM (OPTIONAL)

SALT AND FRESHLY GROUND BLACK PEPPER TO TASTE

2 HANDFULS OAK OR GRAPEVINE WOOD CHIPS, SOAKED IN WATER FOR AT LEAST 30 MINUTES, DRAINED

HEAD-START GRAVY (PAGE 168, OPTIONAL)

1. Build a charcoal fire in an outdoor grill for indirect high grilling (see page 10) and let burn until the coals are almost completely covered with white ash.

2. Meanwhile, starting at the rib cage area on each side of the breast, slip your fingers underneath the turkey skin, loosening it from the flesh, stopping at the center of the breast. Mix the butter, parsley, sage, rosemary, thyme, and marjoram, if using, together in a small bowl. Spread equal amounts of the herb butter underneath the skin on both sides of the breast. Season the turkey with salt and pepper.

3. Toss a handful of chips on the coals. Add 1 cup water to a drip pan. Place the turkey over the drip pan. Cover and grill for 1 hour. Uncover and add 8 briquets to each side of the grill, then sprinkle the remaining chips on the coals. Cover and grill until an instant-read thermometer inserted in the thickest part of the breast not touching a bone reads 170°F, about 30 minutes longer. Transfer the turkey to a platter and let stand for 10 to 15 minutes.

4. Carve the turkey breast and serve with the gravy.

PESTO TURKEY BURGERS WITH FONTINA

MAKES 4 BURGERS
Grilling Method: Banked

When boldly seasoned, turkey burgers can stand up to beef burgers any day of the week. Here, pesto and fontina cheese combine to make **an Italian-inspired burger.** Make your own pesto or use store-bought.

PESTO MAYONNAISE

1/2 CUP MAYONNAISE

2 TABLESPOONS PESTO (PAGE 218), OR USE STORE-BOUGHT

1 1/4 POUNDS GROUND TURKEY

2 TABLESPOONS PESTO (PAGE 218), OR USE STORE-BOUGHT

2 TABLESPOONS DRIED BREAD CRUMBS, PLAIN OR ITALIAN-SEASONED

1 TEASPOON SALT

1/2 TEASPOON FRESHLY GROUND BLACK PEPPER

6 OUNCES FONTINA CHEESE (SEE NOTE), THINLY SLICED

4 HAMBURGER BUNS, SPLIT

1 BEEFSTEAK TOMATO, THINLY SLICED

1. To make the pesto mayonnaise, mix the mayonnaise and pesto together in a small bowl and set aside.

2. Mix the ground turkey, pesto, bread crumbs, salt, and pepper together in a medium bowl. Shape the ground turkey mixture into four patties about 3½ inches across.

3. Build a charcoal fire in an outdoor grill for banked grilling (see page 10), and let burn until the coals are almost completely covered with white ash.

4. Lightly oil the grill grate. Place the turkey burgers over the hotter area of the grill and cover. Cook until the underside is seared with grill marks, about 2 minutes. Turn and repeat with the other side, about 2 minutes longer. Move to the cooler area of the grill, cover, and grill until the burgers feel firm and spring back when pressed in the center, about 6 minutes longer. During the last minute or so, top each burger with equal amounts of sliced cheese, and place the buns on the grill, split sides down, to toast and warm through.

5. To serve, place a burger in a bun and add sliced tomatoes. Serve immediately, with the pesto mayonnaise passed on the side.

Note: The best fontina cheese, with a hint of nuts in its flavor and a creamy texture, comes from the Val d'Aosta region of Italy. Fontinella and domestic fontina are acceptable substitutes.

TIPS FOR TURKEY BURGERS

- There are really three kinds of ground turkey available. Regular ground turkey is made of lean white mean and fattier dark meat together, to get a fat content of about 7 percent. Extra-lean ground turkey is processed from skinless white meat, and comes in at about 1 percent fat. You can also find frozen tubes of ground dark-meal turkey, weighing in at 15 percent fat (about the same as ground round).

- The amount of fat equates to the moisture content of the cooked burger, so the leaner the meat, the drier the burger. Regular ground turkey, with its moderate fat content, is best for burgers, but it still benefits from ingredients that add or hold moisture, such as the pesto and bread crumbs in this recipe.

- As a guard against overcooking and drying out, cook the burgers over the moderate heat of a banked briquet fire. Test by touch, as the burgers are too thin to take an accurate reading with a thermometer. Cook just until the burger bounces back when pressed in the center with a finger.

BUTTERFLIED CORNISH GAME HENS WITH LEMON, ROSEMARY, AND GARLIC

MAKES 2 TO 4 SERVINGS
Grilling Method: Indirect High

One very popular Italian method for grilling poultry is to grill a butterflied (that is, split in half lengthwise and opened up) bird **weighed down with a brick** or some other heavy implement. Such a simple trick exposes the maximum amount of surface to the heat and makes the poultry **cook up fast and juicy.** It works beautifully with Cornish game hens. Whether you serve a half or whole hen per guest depends on their appetites.

TWO 1¼- TO 1½-POUND CORNISH GAME HENS

GRATED ZEST OF 1 LARGE LEMON

3 TABLESPOONS FRESH LEMON JUICE

3 TABLESPOONS EXTRA-VIRGIN OLIVE OIL

2 TEASPOONS DRIED ROSEMARY, OR 4 TEASPOONS CHOPPED FRESH ROSEMARY

2 LARGE GARLIC CLOVES, CRUSHED THROUGH A PRESS

SALT TO TASTE

½ TEASPOON FRESHLY GROUND BLACK PEPPER

1. Using kitchen shears, cut down one side of the backbone of each hen. Open up the hens and place skin sides down on the work surface. Using the heel of your hand, press hard at the breast area to flatten the hen as much as possible.

2. Mix the lemon zest and juice, the oil, rosemary, garlic, salt, and pepper in a large self-sealing plastic bag. Add the hens, close the bag, and turn to coat the hens with the lemon mixture. Let stand at room temperature while lighting the fire. (The hens can be marinated in the refrigerator for up to 8 hours.)

3. Build a charcoal fire in an outdoor grill for indirect high grilling (see page 10), and let burn until the coals are almost completely covered with white ash.

4. Lightly oil the grill grate. Remove the hens from the marinade, reserving the marinade. Place the hens, skin sides down, over a drip pan and pour the marinade on top. Add ½ cup water to the drip pan. Place a foil-wrapped brick or a heavy pot or skillet over each hen. Cover and grill until an instant-read thermometer inserted in the thickest part of the breasts (an easier area to reach on a Cornish hen than the thigh, which is used for larger birds) reads 170°F, about 35 minutes. Remove the bricks. Transfer the hens, skin sides down, to the hotter area of the grill over the coals and cook just until the skin browns and crisps, about 2 minutes. Transfer to a chopping board and let stand 5 minutes. Chop into quarters or halves, and serve hot.

ASIAN DUCK WRAPS WITH HOISIN GLAZE

MAKES 4 WRAPS
Grilling Method: Banked

Boneless duck breast is rich, but also pricey, so luckily a **little goes a long way.** This recipe, **inspired by Beijing duck,** where sliced duck is served in pancakes, makes a light supper, served with a simple Asian vegetable stir-fry on the side.

HOISIN GLAZE

ONE 2-INCH LENGTH FRESH GINGER, SHREDDED ON THE LARGE HOLES OF A BOX GRATER

1/3 CUP PLUS 1 TABLESPOON HOISIN SAUCE

2 TABLESPOONS DRY SHERRY

3 GARLIC CLOVES, CRUSHED THROUGH A PRESS

ONE 14-OUNCE BONELESS MUSCOVY DUCK BREAST (SEE NOTE)

SALT AND FRESHLY GROUND BLACK PEPPER TO TASTE

1 CUCUMBER, PEELED, HALVED LENGTHWISE, SEEDS DISCARDED, CUT INTO THIN HALF-MOONS

2 CUPS SHREDDED NAPA CABBAGE

FOUR 8-INCH-DIAMETER FLOUR TORTILLAS

1. Build a charcoal fire in an outdoor grill for banked grilling (see page 10), and let burn until the coals are almost completely covered with white ash.

2. Meanwhile, make the glaze. In batches, squeeze the shredded ginger in your hand over a small bowl. You should have 2 tablespoons fresh ginger juice. Add the hoisin sauce, sherry, and garlic and mix well.

3. Using a large, sharp knife, cut a crosshatch pattern in the thick skin of the duck breast, being sure not to cut into the flesh. Season the duck breast with salt and pepper.

4. Place the duck, skin side down, over the hotter area of the grill and cover. Grill (there will be flare-ups) until the duck skin is nicely browned, about 3 minutes. The idea here is not just to brown the skin, but to render as much fat as possible at this point. Move the duck breast to the cooler area of the grill, skin side up. Cover and continue cooking for 5 minutes.

Brush the top of the duck with about 2 tablespoons of the hoisin glaze. Reserve the remaining glaze to use as a condiment for the wraps. Cover and cook until the duck breast feels somewhat firmer than raw when pressed, about 5 minutes longer for medium-rare duck. Transfer to a chopping board and let stand for 5 minutes.

5. While the duck cools, arrange the reserved hoisin glaze, cucumber slices, and cabbage on a platter. Grill the tortillas, turning once, until heated through, about 1 minute. Wrap the tortillas in a clean kitchen towel to keep warm.

6. Holding a sharp carving knife at a diagonal, cut the duck into thin slices. Transfer the duck to the platter. Serve, allowing each diner to make a wrap—spread some of the hoisin glaze on a tortilla, add duck and cucumber slices with a sprinkle of cabbage, and roll up the tortilla.

Note: Boneless duck breast is sometimes labeled by its French name, *magret*. There are two varieties on the market: very large Muscovy (almost 1 pound for each half breast), and the smaller Moulard (two 7- to 8-ounce breast halves per package). You can substitute the smaller Moulard for the Muscovy, but after their initial browning, cook them for just 3 minutes, then glaze for another 5 minutes for medium-rare.

SEAFOOD

CEDAR-PLANKED SALMON FILLET WITH HORSERADISH POTATO SALAD

GRILLING CLASSIC

MAKES 4 SERVINGS
Grilling Method: Banked

Long a favorite way to prepare salmon in the Pacific Northwest, cedar-planking is simple—heat a **soaked plank over hot coals** until it is hot, add the fish, and grill in a covered grill. You'll get fish with a sweet-smoky wood flavor and aroma. You can now find wood planks for grill-smoking food everywhere from supermarkets to kitchen shops. While cedar is traditional with salmon, maple or alder, two woods that also come planked for grilling, are excellent, too.

HORSERADISH POTATO SALAD

2 POUNDS RED-SKIN POTATOES, SCRUBBED BUT UNPEELED

2 TABLESPOONS DISTILLED WHITE VINEGAR

½ CUP MAYONNAISE

3 TABLESPOONS PREPARED HORSERADISH

2 SCALLIONS, WHITE AND GREEN PARTS, CHOPPED

2 TABLESPOONS CHOPPED FRESH PARSLEY

SALT AND FRESHLY GROUND BLACK PEPPER TO TASTE

1 CEDAR PLANK FOR SMOKING, SOAKED FOR AT LEAST 30 MINUTES IN COLD WATER TO COVER, DRAINED

ONE 1½-POUND CENTER-CUT SALMON FILLET WITH SKIN

VEGETABLE OIL, FOR BRUSHING

SALT AND FRESHLY GROUND BLACK PEPPER TO TASTE

1. To make the potato salad, place the potatoes in a large saucepan of salted cold water, cover and bring to a boil over high heat. Uncover, reduce the heat to medium-low, and simmer briskly until the potatoes are tender when pierced with a knife, about 25 minutes. Drain the potatoes, rinse under cold water, and transfer to a bowl of iced water to cool.

2. Drain the potatoes and slice them into ½-inch-thick rounds. Place them in a medium bowl and sprinkle with the vinegar. Add the mayonnaise and horseradish and mix gently. Add the scallions and parsley and mix again. Season with salt and pepper. Cover and refrigerate until ready to serve.

3. Build a charcoal fire in an outdoor grill for banked grilling (see page 10) and let burn until the coals are almost completely covered with white ash.

4. Place the drained plank over the hotter area of the grill and heat until the plank is very hot and beginning to scorch at the edges, about 4 minutes. Move the plank to the cooler area of the grill. Brush the salmon on the skin side with the oil and season with salt and pepper. Place the salmon skin side down on the hot plank and cover. Grill (the plank will smolder and darken on the bottom and sides) until the salmon is barely opaque when flaked in the thickest part with the tip of a small knife, 25 to 30 minutes.

5. Transfer the salmon on the plank to a serving platter. Cut into serving portions and serve, with the potato salad.

SWORDFISH WITH RED PEPPER-OLIVE RELISH

MAKES 4 SERVINGS
Grilling Method: Direct Medium

Meaty swordfish isn't afraid of **big, bold flavors.** This chunky red condiment, which is a cross between a salsa (which means sauce in Italian as well as Spanish) and a relish, is bright with such **Mediterranean tastes** as grill-roasted red pepper, olives, garlic, and oregano. Keep this delicious mélange in mind as a bruschetta topping, too.

RED PEPPER-OLIVE RELISH

1 GARLIC CLOVE, CRUSHED UNDER A KNIFE AND PEELED

2 GRILL-ROASTED RED BELL PEPPERS (SEE PAGE 212), PEELED AND COARSELY CHOPPED

½ CUP PITTED KALAMATA OLIVES

1 TABLESPOON EXTRA-VIRGIN OLIVE OIL

1½ TEASPOONS RED WINE VINEGAR

½ TEASPOON DRIED OREGANO

⅛ TEASPOON CRUSHED HOT RED PEPPER

PINCH OF SALT

FOUR 6-OUNCE SWORDFISH STEAKS

OLIVE OIL, FOR BRUSHING

SALT AND FRESHLY GROUND BLACK PEPPER TO TASTE

1. Build a charcoal fire in an outdoor grill for direct medium grilling (see page 8) and let burn until the coals are almost completely covered with white ash.

2. To make the relish, with the machine running, drop the garlic through the feed tube of a food processor fitted with the metal chopping blade to mince it. Add the grilled peppers, olives, oil, vinegar, oregano, hot pepper, and salt, and pulse until the peppers are chopped into ¼-inch dice. Set aside. (The relish can be made up to 3 days ahead, covered and refrigerated. Bring to room temperature before serving.)

3. Lightly oil the grill grate. Lightly brush the swordfish on both sides with the oil and season with salt and pepper. Place the swordfish on the grill and cover. Grill until the underside is lightly browned and seared with grill marks, about 4 minutes. Turn and grill the other side until the swordfish is barely opaque when pierced in the center part with the tip of a small knife, about 4 minutes more.

4. Transfer each swordfish steak to a dinner plate, top with a spoonful of the relish, and serve immediately.

MAHI-MAHI WITH PINEAPPLE-BLUEBERRY SALSA

Mahi-mahi is another firm-textured fish that grills up beautifully. **A tart-sweet fruit salsa** with a bit of habañero chile fire is a fine foil for the briny-fresh flavor of the fish. If you like the salsa spicier, add a little more, but be cautious, as this chile can be incendiary. Make the salsa about an hour before firing up the grill so the ingredients have a chance to mingle.

PINEAPPLE-BLUEBERRY SALSA

1½ CUPS ¼-INCH-DICE FRESH PINEAPPLE

½ CUP FRESH BLUEBERRIES, COARSELY CHOPPED

1 SCALLION, GREEN PART ONLY, FINELY CHOPPED

2 TABLESPOONS CHOPPED FRESH MINT

ZEST OF 1 LIME

2 TABLESPOONS FRESH LIME JUICE

¼ SEEDED AND MINCED HABAÑERO CHILE, OR ½ SEEDED AND MINCED JALAPEÑO

PINCH OF SALT

FOUR 6-OUNCE MAHI-MAHI STEAKS

VEGETABLE OIL, FOR BRUSHING

SALT AND FRESHLY GROUND BLACK PEPPER

1. To make the salsa, combine the pineapple, blueberries, scallion, mint, lime zest and juice, chile, and salt in a small bowl. Cover and let stand at room temperature for at least 1 and up to 4 hours.

2. Build a charcoal fire in an outdoor grill for direct medium grilling (see page 8) and let burn until the coals are almost completely covered with white ash.

3. Lightly oil the grill grate. Lightly brush the mahi-mahi on both sides with the oil and season with salt and pepper. Place the mahi-mahi on the grill and cover. Grill until the underside is lightly browned and seared with grill marks, about 4 minutes. Turn and grill the other side until the swordfish is barely opaque when pierced in the center part with the tip of a small knife, about 4 minutes more.

4. Transfer each mahi-mahi steak to a dinner plate, top with a spoonful of the salsa, and serve immediately.

HONEY-MUSTARD SALMON FILLETS ON MESCLUN

A big salad topped with grilled fish is a satisfying and light supper. Use this banked method for grilling salmon whenever you want to toss it on the grill for a fast weeknight meal. The **honey and mustard topping** will become a favorite.

VINAIGRETTE

2 TABLESPOONS RED WINE VINEGAR

½ TEASPOON GRAINY DIJON-STYLE
    MUSTARD

SALT AND FRESHLY GROUND BLACK PEPPER
    TO TASTE

½ CUP EXTRA-VIRGIN OLIVE OIL

FOUR 7-OUNCE SALMON FILLETS WITH SKIN

VEGETABLE OIL, FOR BRUSHING

SALT AND FRESHLY GROUND BLACK PEPPER
    TO TASTE

3 TABLESPOONS GRAINY DIJON-STYLE
    MUSTARD

1 TABLESPOON HONEY

6 OUNCES MIXED SPRING GREENS
    (MESCLUN)

1 CUP GRAPE OR CHERRY TOMATOES, CUT
    IN HALVES LENGTHWISE

1. Build a charcoal fire in an outdoor grill for banked grilling (see page 10) and let burn until the coals are almost completely covered with white ash.

2. To make the vinaigrette, whisk the vinegar, mustard, salt, and pepper in a small bowl. Gradually whisk in the oil. Set aside.

3. Lightly oil the grill grate. Lightly brush the salmon on both sides with the oil and season with salt and pepper. Place the salmon, flesh side down, over the hottest area of the grill and cover. Grill until the underside is seared with grill marks, about 2 minutes. Move to the cooler side of the grill, skin side down. Mix the mustard and honey together and brush on the salmon. Cover and grill until the salmon is barely opaque when pierced in the thickest part with the tip of a small knife, about 6 minutes. Slip a thin metal spatula between the skin and the grill and transfer the fish to a platter. Don't worry if the skin sticks to the grate.

4. Toss the greens and tomatoes with the vinaigrette in a large bowl. Divide the salad among 4 dinner plates. Top each with a salmon fillet and serve hot.

WHOLE STRIPED BASS WITH FENNEL

MAKES 2 SERVINGS
Grilling Method: Banked

A whole grilled fish makes a **dramatic presentation.** Fish cooked on the bone retains more moisture and is more difficult to overcook. Get out a **fish-grilling basket** (a must) and get cooking.

ONE 12-OUNCE FENNEL BULB, WITH FRONDS

EXTRA-VIRGIN OLIVE OIL, FOR BRUSHING, PLUS MORE FOR SERVING

SALT AND FRESHLY GROUND BLACK PEPPER TO TASTE

1 LARGE LEMON, HALF THINLY SLICED, AND REMAINDER CUT INTO WEDGES

ONE 1½-POUND WHOLE STRIPED BASS, CLEANED, WELL RINSED, AND DRIED

1. Cut the green fronds from the fennel and set them aside. Cut the fennel lengthwise into ½-inch-thick slices. Lightly brush the fennel slices with oil and season with salt and pepper.

2. Using a thin sharp knife, score two shallow slits about 2 inches apart in the meatiest part of the fish; turn and repeat on the other side. Place the fennel fronds and lemon slices in the body cavity. Brush the outside of the fish with olive oil and season inside and out with salt and pepper. Place in a well-oiled fish basket and clip the basket closed.

3. Build a charcoal fire in an outdoor grill for banked grilling (see page 10) and let burn until the coals are almost completely covered with white ash.

4. Lightly oil the grill grate. Place the fish basket over the hotter area of the grill—you will not be able to cover the grill. Grill until the underside of the fish is golden brown, about 5 minutes. Turn the fish. Place the fennel slices on the cooler area of the grill. Grill, turning the fennel occasionally, until the fish is golden brown on the other side, the meat in the slits looks opaque, and the fennel is crisp-tender, about 5 minutes longer.

6. Remove the fish from the basket and transfer to a platter. Surround the fish with the fennel slices and the lemon wedges. To serve, run the tip of a sharp knife around the perimeter of the fish. Use a fork to gently separate the upper fillet from the bone. Slide the knife under the fillet and transfer to a dinner plate. Pull the tail up, and the bone structure and head will come away from the bottom fillet; discard the bones and head. Transfer the bottom fillet to a dinner plate. Drizzle each fillet with olive oil. Serve hot, with the fennel and lemons.

RAINBOW TROUT WITH SPINACH-PINE NUT STUFFING

MAKES 4 SERVINGS
Grilling Method: Direct Medium

Individual rainbow trout are sophisticated enough for dinner party fare, but this stuffing is so easy to make that you might think about it for a weeknight dinner, too. If you like grilling trout, you'll want to get **a grilling basket that holds four fish,** as the basket will make turning the fish much easier.

STUFFING

¼ CUP PINE NUTS

2 TABLESPOONS UNSALTED BUTTER

2 TABLESPOONS CHOPPED SHALLOTS

1 GARLIC CLOVE, FINELY CHOPPED

ONE 10-OUNCE BOX THAWED FROZEN SPINACH, SQUEEZED WITH YOUR HANDS TO REMOVE EXCESS MOISTURE

½ CUP FRESH BREAD CRUMBS

SALT AND FRESHLY GROUND BLACK PEPPER TO TASTE

FOUR 12-OUNCE RAINBOW TROUT, CLEANED

SALT AND FRESHLY GROUND BLACK PEPPER TO TASTE

LEMON WEDGES, FOR SERVING

1. Build a charcoal fire in an outdoor grill for direct medium grilling (see page 8) and let burn until the coals are almost completely covered with white ash.

2. Meanwhile, make the stuffing. Heat an empty medium skillet over medium heat. Add the pine nuts and cook, stirring often, until toasted, about 1 minute. Transfer to a bowl. Add the butter to the skillet and melt. Add the shallots and cook until softened, about 1 minute. Stir in the garlic and cook until fragrant, about 1 minute more. Add the spinach and stir to evaporate excess moisture in the spinach, about 1 minute. Transfer to the bowl and add the bread crumbs. Mix and season with salt and pepper.

3. Score both sides of each trout with 2 shallow slashes about 1 inch apart. Season the trout lightly with salt and pepper inside and out. Fill the body cavity of each trout with the stuffing. Do not worry about closing up the trout with wooden skewers. Lightly oil a fish basket with 4 compartments, place the trout in the basket, and clip it closed.

4. Lightly oil the grill grate. Place the basket on the grill and cover. Grill until the trout are lightly browned and the meat in the slashes looks opaque, about 4 minutes. Turn, cover, and grill the other side, about 4 minutes more.

5. Remove the trout from the basket and place 1 trout on each of 4 dinner plates. Serve immediately with the lemon wedges.

TUNA WITH CHOPPED SALAD NIÇOISE

MAKES 4 SERVINGS
Grilling Method: Direct High

This deconstructed version of Niçoise salad takes all of the **familiar elements**—tomatoes, green beans, potatoes, olives, and hard-boiled eggs—and chops them into a colorful side dish for grilled (not canned!) tuna. While most fish steaks are best cooked over moderate heat, tuna shines when it is **seared over very hot heat.**

CHOPPED SALAD NIÇOISE

1½ POUNDS RED-SKIN POTATOES, SCRUBBED BUT NOT PEELED

6 OUNCES GREEN BEANS, TRIMMED AND CUT INTO ½-INCH LENGTHS

1 TABLESPOON RED WINE VINEGAR

SALT AND FRESHLY GROUND BLACK PEPPER TO TASTE

¼ CUP EXTRA-VIRGIN OLIVE OIL

2 HARD-BOILED EGGS, PEELED AND CHOPPED (SEE NOTE)

1 MEDIUM TOMATO, SEEDED AND DICED

¼ CUP CHOPPED PITTED KALAMATA OLIVES

FOUR 6-OUNCE TUNA STEAKS

EXTRA-VIRGIN OLIVE OIL, FOR BRUSHING

SALT AND FRESHLY GROUND BLACK PEPPER TO TASTE

1. To make the salad, place the potatoes in a large saucepan of salted water and bring to a boil over high heat. Cook until the potatoes are tender when pierced with the tip of a sharp knife, about 25 minutes; during the last 4 minutes, add the green beans so they can cook along with the potatoes until the beans are crisp-tender. Drain the potatoes and green beans and rinse under cold running water. Transfer to a bowl of iced water to cool.

2. Drain the potatoes and green beans. Slice the potatoes into ½-inch rounds. Whisk the vinegar, salt, and pepper in a small bowl and gradually whisk in the oil. Add the potatoes, green beans, eggs, tomato, and olives and mix well. Adjust the seasoning with salt and pepper. Cover and refrigerate until ready to serve. (The salad is best the day it is made.)

3. Build a charcoal fire in an outdoor grill for direct high grilling (see page 8) and let burn until the coals are almost completely covered with white ash.

4. Lightly oil the grill grate. Lightly brush the tuna on both sides with the oil and season with salt and pepper. Place the tuna on the grill and cover. Grill until the underside is lightly browned and seared with grill marks, about 1½ minutes. Turn and grill the other side until the exterior of the tuna is opaque to a depth of about ½ inch when pierced with the tip of a small knife (it will look red beyond the opaque area), about 1½ minutes more.

5. Transfer each tuna steak to a dinner plate, add a serving of the chopped salad, and serve immediately.

Note: The best way to hard-boil eggs is to not boil them at all. Overcooking creates a discolored green ring around the yolk and gives the eggs a sulfurous smell. To cook hard-boiled eggs, place the eggs in a small saucepan and add enough cold water to cover. Bring to a simmer over high heat. Remove from the heat, cover, and let stand for 15 minutes. The residual heat will cook the eggs perfectly. Drain the eggs, run under cold water to cool, then peel and use as needed.

FISH TACOS WITH GARLICKY SLAW

MAKES 8 TACOS, 4 SERVINGS
Grilling Method: Direct Medium

There's more than one way to make a fish taco. If you're used to the deep-fried version, try this **much lighter but equally delectable rendition.** Cod is one of the sweetest fish around, but it could fall apart a bit when you turn it on the grill. You could use a perforated grilling screen, but it actually makes no difference, because the fish will be chunked before serving, anyway.

GARLICKY SLAW

1/2 CUP MAYONNAISE

GRATED ZEST OF 1 LIME

2 TABLESPOONS FRESH LIME JUICE

1 LARGE GARLIC CLOVE, CRUSHED THROUGH
   A PRESS

1 POUND COLESLAW MIX

SALT AND FRESHLY GROUND BLACK PEPPER
   TO TASTE

1 1/2 POUNDS COD FILLET

EXTRA-VIRGIN OLIVE OIL, FOR BRUSHING

1 TEASPOON CHILI POWDER

SALT TO TASTE

8 SMALL 7-INCH CORN TORTILLAS

STORE-BOUGHT TOMATO SALSA, FOR
   SERVING

1. To make the slaw, whisk the mayonnaise, lime zest and juice, and garlic in a medium bowl. Add the cole slaw mix and mix well. Season with salt and pepper. Cover and let stand while building the fire. (The slaw can be made, covered and refrigerated, 1 day ahead. Let stand at room temperature for 1 hour before serving.)

2. Build a charcoal fire in an outdoor grill for direct medium grilling (see page 8) and let burn until the coals are almost completely covered with white ash.

3. Lightly oil the grill grate. Lightly brush the cod with the oil and season with the chili powder and salt. Place the cod on the grill and cover. Grill until the underside is lightly browned and seared with grill marks, about 5 minutes. Turn and grill the other side until the cod is just opaque in the thickest exterior when pierced with the tip of a small knife, about 5 minutes more. During the last couple of minutes, add the tortillas to the grill and grill, turning once, until heated through. Transfer the cod to a serving bowl and break up with a fork into large flakes. Transfer the tortillas to a cloth-lined basket or bowl and wrap in the cloth to keep them warm.

4. Serve the fish, tortillas, slaw, and salsa, allowing each guest to roll up the fish, slaw, and salsa in a tortilla to make each taco.

PIRI-PIRI SHRIMP AND SAUSAGE SKEWERS

MAKES 4 SERVINGS
Grilling Method: Banked

Piri-Piri, the **incendiary** Portuguese hot sauce, makes a delicious coating for shrimp, which are then skewered with garlicky sausage and red bell peppers to create an interplay of sweet and spicy. Use the largest shrimp you can find, preferably the ones designated U-15s (for "under fifteen to a pound"), for if the shrimp are too small, they will overcook by the time the **sausage sizzles.** Serve them on a bed of cool salad greens.

16 COLOSSAL OR JUMBO (U-15) SHRIMP, PEELED AND DEVEINED

¼ CUP PIRI-PIRI (PAGE 46), PLUS MORE FOR SERVING

9 OUNCES HARD SMOKED SAUSAGE, SUCH AS LINGUIÇA OR CHORIZO, CUT INTO 16 ROUNDS ABOUT
¾ INCH THICK

1 LARGE RED BELL PEPPER, SEEDS AND RIBS REMOVED, CUT INTO 16 PIECES ABOUT 1 INCH SQUARE

1 TABLESPOON RED WINE VINEGAR

SALT AND FRESHLY GROUND BLACK PEPPER TO TASTE

¼ CUP EXTRA-VIRGIN OLIVE OIL

6 CUPS MIXED GREENS, SUCH AS MESCLUN

1. Combine the shrimp and piri-piri in a resealable plastic bag. Refrigerate while building the fire or no longer than 1 hour.

2. Build a charcoal fire in an outdoor grill for banked grilling (see page 10) and let it burn until the coals are almost completely covered with white ash.

3. On each of 4 metal skewers, thread 1 shrimp, 1 piece of sausage, and 1 piece of red bell pepper. When threading the shrimp, hold them in their natural C shape, then thread them on the skewer from top to bottom to retain this shape. Repeat with the remaining shrimp, sausage, and bell pepper, using a total of 4 each for each skewer. Do not crowd the ingredients on the skewer. Discard the piri-piri in the plastic bag.

4. Lightly oil the grilling grate. Place the kebabs over the cooler side of the grill and cover. Cook, turning occasionally, until the shrimp is firm and opaque and the edges of the sausage are sizzling, about 6 minutes.

5. Whisk the vinegar, salt, and pepper. Gradually whisk in the olive oil. Add the greens and toss well. Divide the salad among 4 salad plates. Slide the shrimp, sausage, and pepper from each skewer onto each plate. Serve hot, with the remaining piri-piri for dipping.

BOURBON-GLAZED SHRIMP ON COLD SESAME NOODLES

MAKES 6 SERVINGS
Grilling Method: Direct High

With sweet and sticky shrimp topping a cool mound of Asian noodle salad, this recipe make use of one of the most helpful of all grilling accessories, **the grilling grid.** Placed on top of the grill's cooking grate, it will keep shrimp and other small food from falling into the coals. When preparing the ginger and garlic for the glaze, use a large, sharp knife to get distinct pieces that retain their shape, and resist the temptation to use a food processor. While noodles and dressing can be prepared ahead, do not mix them together until just before serving, or the noodles will get stodgy. The original Chinese recipe uses sesame paste for the dressing, but peanut butter works just fine.

COLD SESAME NOODLES

1 POUND CHINESE EGG NOODLES OR DRIED LINGUINE

1 TABLESPOON ASIAN DARK SESAME OIL OR VEGETABLE OIL

½ CUP SMOOTH PEANUT BUTTER

2 TABLESPOONS SOY SAUCE

2 TABLESPOONS BALSAMIC VINEGAR

2 TABLESPOONS BOURBON

1 TABLESPOON HOT SESAME OIL

2 TEASPOONS SUGAR

2 SCALLIONS, WHITE PARTS MINCED, GREEN PARTS CHOPPED, RESERVED SEPARATELY

2 GARLIC CLOVES, CRUSHED THROUGH A PRESS

2 TABLESPOONS BOURBON

2 TABLESPOONS SOY SAUCE

2 TABLESPOONS MOLASSES

2 GARLIC CLOVES, MINCED

1 TABLESPOON PEELED AND MINCED GINGER

½ TEASPOON FRESHLY GROUND BLACK PEPPER

1½ POUNDS LARGE (21–25) SHRIMP, PEELED AND DEVEINED

1 CUCUMBER, PEELED, HALVED LENGTHWISE, SEEDS REMOVED, AND CUT INTO THIN HALF-MOONS

2 LARGE CARROTS, SHREDDED

2 TEASPOONS SESAME SEEDS, TOASTED (SEE PAGE 159)

1. Bring a large pot of lightly salted water to a boil over high heat. Add the noodles and cook until tender, about 8 minutes. Drain and rinse under cold running water until cool. Drain again and toss with the sesame oil. (The noodles can be covered and refrigerated for up to 6 hours.)

2. To make the dressing, whisk the peanut butter, soy sauce, vinegar, bourbon, hot oil, and sugar together in a medium bowl. Add the white parts of the scallions and the garlic. Add ½ cup water and whisk until smooth. (The dressing can be covered and stored at room temperature for up to 6 hours. Do not refrigerate.)

3. Build a charcoal fire in an outdoor grill for direct high grilling (see page 8) and let it burn until the coals are almost completely covered with white ash.

4. Whisk the bourbon, soy sauce, molasses, garlic, ginger, and black pepper together in a medium bowl. Add the shrimp and mix well. Cover and refrigerate while building the fire.

5. Place a perforated grilling grate on the grill's cooking grate. Lightly oil the top grate. Spread the shrimp on the grate and cover. Cook for 2 minutes. Turn the shrimp, cover, and grill until they are firm and opaque, about 2 minutes longer.

6. Mix the noodles and dressing in a large bowl and transfer to a deep platter. Top with the cucumbers and carrots, then the shrimp. Sprinkle with the green parts of the scallions, then the sesame seeds. Serve at once.

SEA SCALLOPS WITH ORANGE-TARRAGON BUTTER SAUCE

MAKES 4 SERVINGS
Grilling Method: Banked

This is the recipe to make when you find **perfect scallops** at the best fish store in town. They will look glistening and plump, but be sure that the store assures you that they have not been soaked in any preserving chemicals, which gives them an off flavor. **A classic butter sauce** gives them the finishing touch. Serve them with steamed rice and a simple green vegetable, perhaps sautéed snow peas.

ORANGE-TARRAGON BUTTER SAUCE

1 CUP DRY WHITE WINE, SUCH AS PINOT GRIGIO

2 TABLESPOONS WHITE WINE VINEGAR

2 TABLESPOONS CHOPPED SHALLOTS

1 CUP (2 STICKS) UNSALTED BUTTER, CUT INTO 16 EQUAL PIECES, CHILLED

ZEST OF 1 ORANGE

1 TEASPOON CHOPPED FRESH TARRAGON

SALT AND FRESHLY GROUND BLACK PEPPER TO TASTE

16 LARGE (2 POUNDS) SEA SCALLOPS

VEGETABLE OIL, FOR BRUSHING

SALT AND FRESHLY GROUND BLACK PEPPER TO TASTE

1. Build a charcoal fire in an outdoor grill for banked grilling (see page 10) and let burn until the coals are almost completely covered with white ash.

2. Meanwhile, make the sauce. Bring the wine, vinegar, and shallots to a boil in a small saucepan over high heat. Cook until the liquid has reduced to about 2 tablespoons, about 10 minutes. Reduce the heat to very low. Whisk in the butter, one piece at a time, whisking until each piece is almost incorporated before adding the next piece. The butter should soften into an ivory sauce—it should not melt. Occasionally remove the saucepan from the stove to monitor the heat. Work quickly, as it should take you only a couple of minutes to make the sauce. (For a smoother sauce, you may strain it through a wire sieve into a small heatproof bowl.) Stir in the orange zest and tarragon, and season with salt and pepper. Transfer the saucepan to a skillet of very hot, not simmering, water, to keep warm for up to 30 minutes. (Or transfer the sauce to a wide-mouthed vacuum canister to store for up to 2 hours.) The sauce does not need to be piping hot, as it will heat when it comes into contact with the hot scallops.

3. Lightly oil the grill grate. Lightly brush the scallops with oil and season with salt and pepper. Place the scallops over the hotter area of the grill and cover. Cook until the undersides are seared with grill marks, about 2 minutes. Turn, cover, and sear the other sides, about 2 minutes more. Move to the cooler area of the grill and cover. Grill until the scallops feel firm when pressed, about 3 minutes longer.

4. Spoon equal amounts of the sauce on 4 dinner plates. Top each with 4 scallops and serve.

BIG EASY CRAB CAKES WITH REMOULADE

MAKES 6 SERVINGS
Grilling Method: Direct Medium

These plump, sweet, and spicy crab cakes will bring to mind **great memories of New Orleans** and inspire new good times to come. Remoulade, a tartar sauce on steroids, is used as not only a sauce, but also a moistener/flavoring in the crabmeat mixture. These crab cakes can be served with a small green salad as an appetizer, on a roll as a sandwich, or with slaw as a main course.

REMOULADE

1¼ CUPS MAYONNAISE

1 TABLESPOON CREOLE, SPICY YELLOW, OR DIJON MUSTARD

½ TEASPOON HOT RED PEPPER SAUCE

¼ CUP CHOPPED CORNICHONS (TINY SOUR PICKLES) OR DILL GHERKINS

3 TABLESPOONS DRAINED AND RINSED NONPAREIL CAPERS

3 TABLESPOONS CHOPPED PITTED GREEN OLIVES

3 TABLESPOONS CHOPPED FRESH PARSLEY

CRAB CAKES

1 LARGE EGG, BEATEN

1 TEASPOON CAJUN SEASONING (SEE NOTE), OR USE STORE-BOUGHT, SALT-FREE CAJUN OR CREOLE SEASONING

1 TEASPOON WORCESTERSHIRE SAUCE

¼ TEASPOON SALT

1 POUND CRABMEAT, PICKED OVER FOR SHELLS AND CARTILAGE

1 CUP DRIED BREAD CRUMBS, DIVIDED

⅓ CUP FINELY CHOPPED RED BELL PEPPER

1. To make the remoulade, mix the mayonnaise, mustard, and hot pepper sauce in a small bowl. Add the cornichons, capers, olives, and parsley and mix well. Cover and refrigerate until ready to use. (The remoulade can be made up to 3 days ahead.)

2. To make the crab cakes, mix ½ cup of the remoulade, egg, the Cajun seasoning, Worcestershire sauce, and salt in a medium bowl. Add the crabmeat, ½ cup of the bread crumbs, and the bell pepper and mix. Cover and refrigerate for 30 minutes. Transfer the remaining remoulade to a serving bowl, cover, and refrigerate until ready to serve.

3. Form the crab cakes into six 3-inch diameter patties. Spread the remaining ½ cup bread crumbs in a shallow dish. Coat the patties in the bread crumbs, transfer to a plate, cover and refrigerate for at least 30 minutes and up to 4 hours.

4. Build a charcoal fire in an outdoor grill for direct medium grilling (see page 8) and let burn until the coals are almost completely covered with white ash.

5. Lightly oil the grill grate. Place the crab cakes on the grill and cover. Cook until the underside is golden brown, about 4 minutes. Turn, cover, and grill until the other side is golden brown, about 4 minutes longer.

6. Transfer the crab cakes to individual dinner plates and serve, with the remaining remoulade passed on the side.

Note: To make your own Cajun seasoning, mix 2 tablespoons sweet Hungarian paprika, 1 tablespoon each dried basil and dried thyme, 1 teaspoon each garlic powder and onion powder, ½ teaspoon freshly ground black pepper, and ⅛ teaspoon cayenne pepper. Store in an airtight container in a cool, dark place for up to 6 months.

BUTTERFLIED LOBSTER TAIL WITH SHALLOTS AND HERBS

MAKES 2 SERVINGS
Grilling Method: Direct Medium

Grilled lobster sounds enticing, but it is quite a challenge to deal with a big unwieldy crustacean. Lobster tail solves the problem. The tail is opened up like a book to expose the flesh to the heat of the grill, searing in moisture. **Herb-flecked butter** adds another layer of **indulgent flavor.**

6 TABLESPOONS (¾ STICK) UNSALTED BUTTER, CUT UP

2 TEASPOONS FINELY CHOPPED SHALLOT

1 TEASPOON FINELY CHOPPED FRESH TARRAGON

1 TEASPOON FINELY CHOPPED FRESH CHIVES

TWO 9-INCH THAWED FROZEN LOBSTER TAILS

SALT AND FRESHLY GROUND BLACK PEPPER TO TASTE

LEMON WEDGES, FOR SERVING

1. Build a charcoal fire in an outdoor grill for direct grilling (see page 8) and let burn until the coals are almost completely covered with white ash.

2. Melt the butter in a small saucepan over medium heat. Reserve 1 tablespoon in a small bowl. Pour the remaining butter into another small bowl. Stir in the shallot, tarragon, and chives and set aside.

3. Using kitchen scissors, snip down the center of the underside of each lobster tail. Using a large sharp knife, cut through the lobster flesh down to, but do not cut through, the top of the shell. Open up each tail like a book. Brush the flesh of the tails with the reserved plain melted butter and season with salt and pepper.

4. Lightly oil the grill grate. Place the tails, flesh sides down, on the grill and cover. Grill until the undersides are lightly browned and seared with grill marks, about 3 minutes. Transfer the lobster tails onto dinner plates. Spoon the herb butter into each shell and serve immediately, with the lemon wedges.

VEGETABLES

ARTICHOKES WITH ROASTED GARLIC AÏOLI

MAKES 4 SERVINGS
Grilling Method: Banked

Artichokes are often boiled in copious amounts of water, a method that is efficient but leaves plenty of flavor in the pot. However, when the green globes are **wrapped in foil** and grilled, they cook in their own juices, intensifying their taste. Roasted Garlic Aïoli is a great dip for the tender leaves, but so is Romesco Sauce (page 208), melted butter, or your favorite vinaigrette.

4 MEDIUM ARTICHOKES

2 LEMONS, HALVED

8 TEASPOONS EXTRA-VIRGIN OLIVE OIL

4 GARLIC CLOVES, COARSELY CHOPPED

SALT AND FRESHLY GROUND BLACK PEPPER TO TASTE

ROASTED GARLIC AÏOLI (PAGE 64)

1. Build a charcoal fire in an outdoor grill for banked grilling (see page 10) and let burn until the coals are almost completely covered with white ash.

2. Tear off four 16-inch lengths of heavy-duty aluminum foil. Using kitchen shears, snip off the thorny tips from the artichoke leaves. Place an artichoke in the center of a foil rectangle. Squeeze the juice of half a lemon on the artichoke, drizzle with 2 teaspoons of oil, sprinkle with 1 chopped garlic clove, and season with salt and pepper. Wrap the artichoke in the foil to completely enclose it. If using regular foil, wrap with a second piece of foil to make a double thickness. Repeat with the remaining artichokes.

3. Place the artichokes over the cooler area of the grill and cover. Grill, turning occasionally, until an artichoke leaf pulls easily away from the base (open the foil to check), about 40 minutes. Serve hot, with the mayonnaise, and a bowl to hold the used leaves.

ACORN SQUASH WITH ORANGE-CHIPOTLE GLAZE

MAKES 4 SERVINGS
Grilling Method: Indirect High

Grilling foil-wrapped acorn squash concentrates the squash's natural sugars. An easy glaze of orange marmalade and chipotle chile **accents the sweetness.** Try this as a side dish for grilled pork, which can be cooked over the hotter area of the grill, yielding two dishes from the same batch of coals.

1 ACORN SQUASH, ABOUT 1¼ POUNDS

SALT TO TASTE

¼ CUP ORANGE MARMALADE, PREFERABLY BITTER ORANGE

½ CANNED CHIPOTLE CHILE IN ADOBO, MINCED WITH ANY CLINGING SAUCE, OR MORE TO TASTE

2 TABLESPOONS UNSALTED BUTTER, CUT INTO BITS

1. Build a charcoal fire in an outdoor grill for indirect high grilling (see page 10) and let burn until the coals are almost completely covered with white ash. You will not need a drip pan.

2. Cut the squash in half lengthwise through the stem. Scoop out the seeds. Season the cut surface with salt. Wrap each squash half in heavy-duty aluminum foil. If using regular foil, wrap with another piece of foil to make a double thickness. Mix the marmalade and chipotle together in a small bowl and set aside.

3. Place the squash, cut sides up, over the cooler area of the grill and cover. Grill until the squash is barely tender when pierced with the tip of a small sharp knife (unwrap to check), about 45 minutes.

4. Transfer the squash to a baking sheet. Remove the foil and pour out any liquid that has collected in the hollow of each squash half. Brush the marmalade mixture over the cut sides of the squash and dot with the butter. Return to the grill, cut sides up, and cover. Grill until the glaze is bubbling, 7 to 10 minutes.

5. Transfer the squash to a cutting board. Cut each squash half crosswise with a large knife to make 4 pieces. Serve hot.

CHIPOTLE CHILES

Chipotle chiles are jalapenōs that have been dried over a fire, which intensifies their heat and gives them a smoky flavor. They're available dried whole, dried and ground into a powder, and canned with a chile sauce called adobo. This recipe uses the canned variety. Transfer any leftover chiles with their sauce to a covered plastic container and refrigerate for up to 2 weeks. Or place the individual chiles with any clinging sauce on a waxed paper–lined baking sheet, and freeze until the chiles are solid. Transfer the frozen chiles and their sauce to an airtight container and freeze to store for up to 3 months—you can defrost the frozen chiles one at a time as needed. It's a good idea to take care when handling any chile, but be extra cautious with chipotles, as they are especially spicy and their sauce makes it even easier to transfer the heat to delicate parts of your body.

ASPARAGUS WITH ROMESCO SAUCE

MAKES 4 SERVINGS
Grilling Method: Direct High

Many cooks love **grilled asparagus** so much that they won't even consider going back to boiling or steaming their spears. Be sure to place the asparagus perpendicular to the grill grid, or they will fall through the grate. To thwart disaster, use a perforated grilling screen over the grate to contain the asparagus. And be flexible with the timing, as thicker spears will take a bit longer than thin ones, of course. Bold Romesco is the perfect sauce.

ROMESCO SAUCE

¼ CUP SLICED NATURAL ALMONDS

1 LARGE GARLIC CLOVE, CRUSHED UNDER A KNIFE AND PEELED

2 GRILLED RED BELL PEPPERS (PAGE 212), SKINS AND SEEDS REMOVED

2 TEASPOONS SHERRY OR RED WINE VINEGAR

1 TEASPOON SWEET PAPRIKA, PREFERABLY SMOKED SPANISH PAPRIKA, SUCH AS PIMENTÓN DE LA VERA

½ TEASPOON DRIED OREGANO

3 TABLESPOONS EXTRA-VIRGIN OLIVE OIL

SALT AND FRESHLY GROUND BLACK PEPPER TO TASTE

1 TABLESPOON EXTRA-VIRGIN OLIVE OIL, AS NEEDED

1 POUND ASPARAGUS

1. To make the Romesco sauce, heat an empty skillet over medium heat. Add the almonds and cook, stirring often, until toasted, about 2 minutes. Transfer to a plate to cool.

2. With the machine running, drop the garlic through the feed tube of a food processor fitted with the metal chopping blade to chop it. Add the red peppers, vinegar, paprika, and oregano. Gradually add the oil, then season with the salt and pepper. Transfer the sauce to a serving bowl. (The sauce can be made up to 5 days ahead, covered and refrigerated. Bring to room temperature before serving.)

3. Build a charcoal fire in an outdoor grill for direct high grilling (see page 8) and let burn until the coals are almost completely covered with white ash.

4. Drizzle the oil on a rimmed baking sheet. Spread the asparagus on the sheet and roll in the oil to coat lightly, adding a bit more oil if needed. Do not add too much oil, or it will drip on the coals and cause flare-ups.

5. Lightly oil the grill grate. Place the asparagus perpendicular to the grill grid. Grill uncovered, occasionally rolling the asparagus on the grill to turn them, until the asparagus is seared with grill marks and crisp-tender, about 3 minutes. Transfer the asparagus to a platter and serve hot or cooled to room temperature, with the sauce.

CORN ON THE COB WITH SPICY LIME BUTTER

MAKES 4 SERVINGS
Grilling Method: Direct High

There's nothing to grilling corn on the cob—just put the unhusked ears over the coals and grill them until the husks are charred. The moisture in the husks and silks will create steam to cook the kernels, so there's **no need to soak the corn** in water first. As the grilling itself is so simple, you'll have extra time to whip up **a special butter** for slathering onto the hot corn.

SPICY LIME BUTTER

8 TABLESPOONS (1 STICK) UNSALTED BUTTER, SOFTENED

GRATED ZEST OF 1 LIME

1 CANNED CHIPOTLE CHILE IN ADOBO SAUCE WITH ANY
    CLINGING SAUCE, MINCED

SALT TO TASTE

4 EARS OF CORN, UNHUSKED

1. To make the butter, mash the butter, lime zest, and chile in a small bowl with a rubber spatula until combined. Season with salt to taste. Transfer the butter to a serving bowl and set aside at room temperature. (The butter can be made up to 1 week ahead, covered and refrigerated. Bring to room temperature before serving.)

2. Build a charcoal fire in an outdoor grill for direct high grilling (see page 8) and let burn until the coals are almost completely covered with white ash.

3. Place the corn on the grill and cover. Grill, turning occasionally, until the husks are charred on all sides, about 20 minutes. Transfer the corn to a platter.

4. Using a clean kitchen towel to protect your hands, strip off the husks and silks. Serve hot, with the butter passed on the side.

RED PEPPERS AND GOAT CHEESE WITH OREGANO VINAIGRETTE

MAKES 4 TO 6 SERVINGS
Grilling Method: Direct High

Knowing how to grill peppers is **one of the most useful techniques** a grill chef can master. There are many recipes that call for cooked, peeled peppers, such as Romesco Sauce, on page 208. Grilling not only blackens the skin to make it easier to remove but also flavors the flesh as it cooks. By the way, you do not need to cover the grilled peppers while they cool—in fact, the steam will continue to cook them making them softer and more difficult to peel. **This colorful salad can play many roles.** Serve it as a side dish to grilled chicken, or as part of an antipasto selection. It can also do duty as an appetizer, served on grilled slices of crusty bread.

4 RED BELL PEPPERS, PREPARED FOR GRILLING (SEE "PREPPING GRILLED PEPPERS," PAGE 213)

1 TABLESPOON RED WINE VINEGAR

1 TEASPOON DRIED OREGANO

1 LARGE GARLIC CLOVE, FINELY CHOPPED

SALT AND FRESHLY GROUND BLACK PEPPER TO TASTE

¼ CUP EXTRA-VIRGIN OLIVE OIL

½ CUP (2 OUNCES) CRUMBLED RINDLESS GOAT CHEESE (CHÈVRE)

1. Build a charcoal fire in an outdoor grill for direct high grilling (see page 8) and let burn until the coals are almost completely covered with white ash.

2. Place the peppers on the grill, skin sides down, and cover. Grill until the skin is blistered and charred, about 5 minutes. Take care to grill just until the skins are blackened and do not grill a hole through the flesh.

3. Cool the peppers until easy to handle. Remove and discard the charred skin. You can use a small knife to help scrape off stubborn areas of skin, but do not work under running water, which only serves to rinse away flavor. If absolutely necessary, you can give the skinned peppers a very quick pass under cold water to rinse away bits of blackened skin. Remove the seeds and discard. Cut the peppers lengthwise into 2- to 3-inch-wide strips. Arrange the strips on a platter.

4. Whisk the vinegar, oregano, garlic, salt, and pepper in a small bowl. Gradually whisk in the oil. Drizzle over the peppers and sprinkle with the goat cheese. Serve immediately.

PREPPING GRILLED PEPPERS

Some cooks grill whole peppers, which means turning them often until they are charred on all sides. There is an easier way—open up the peppers into a long strip and they won't need constant attention during grilling. To prepare red peppers for grilling, cut off the top and bottom of each pepper to make "lids." Cut each pepper down the side and open up into a large strip. Cut away the ribs and seeds. The strip and lids can be grilled over charcoal to blacken the skin and ready it for removing.

PORTOBELLO, RED PEPPER, AND FONTINA SANDWICH

MAKES 4 SANDWICHES
Grilling Method: Banked

Big portobello mushrooms are at their very best when lightly marinated and grilled to develop **a toothsome, meaty texture and earthy flavor.** They can stand up to bold accents like zesty roasted pepper, garlicky aïoli, and rich fontina cheese, all of which join the mushrooms in these toasty sandwiches.

FOUR 3-OUNCE PORTOBELLO MUSHROOM CAPS, STEMS TRIMMED

2 TABLESPOONS BALSAMIC VINEGAR

¼ TEASPOON SALT

¼ TEASPOON FRESHLY GROUND BLACK PEPPER

½ CUP EXTRA-VIRGIN OLIVE OIL

1 LARGE RED BELL PEPPER, PREPARED FOR GRILLING (SEE "PREPPING GRILLED PEPPERS," PAGE 213)

4 OUNCES FONTINA, THINLY SLICED

8 SLICES RUSTIC-STYLE BREAD

½ CUP ROASTED GARLIC AÏOLI (PAGE 64)

16 LARGE ARUGULA LEAVES

1. Wipe the mushrooms clean with a wet paper towel. Whisk the vinegar, salt, and pepper in a small bowl, then whisk in the oil. Transfer to a resealable plastic bag, add the mushrooms, and turn to coat well. Let stand at room temperature while building the fire.

2. Build a charcoal fire in an outdoor grill for banked grilling (see page 10) and let burn until the coals are almost completely covered with white ash. You will not need a drip pan.

3. Lightly oil the grill grate. Remove the mushrooms from the marinade and drain well, reserving the marinade. Place the mushrooms, gill sides up, over the hotter area of the grill. Add the pepper, skin side down, next to the mushrooms and cover:

- Red bell pepper: Grill until the skin is blackened and charred, about 5 minutes. Transfer to a plate and let stand until cool enough to handle. Remove and discard the skin. Cut the pepper into 4 equal pieces.

- Mushrooms: Grill until the undersides are lightly browned, about 2 minutes. Turn and move to the cooler area of the grill. Pour the reserved marinade over the mushrooms, taking care that the marinade does not splash onto the ashes. Cover and grill until the mushrooms are tender, about 8 minutes. During the last 2 minutes, top each mushroom with equal amounts of the fontina cheese.

When you add the cheese to the mushrooms, place the bread slices on the grill grate and grill, turning once, until toasted on both sides, about 2 minutes.

4. Spread the aïoli on the toasted bread. Place 4 slices, aïoli sides up, on a work surface. Top each with a mushroom, a piece of red pepper, and 4 arugula leaves. Top with the remaining bread slices, aïoli sides down. Cut each sandwich in half and serve hot.

RADICCHIO WITH OLIO SANTO

On many tables in Tuscany you'll find cruets of *olio santo* (holy oil) to **anoint food** with a drizzle of **spicy, herbaceous flavor.** Here it perks up another Italian favorite, radicchio, which is surprisingly good grilled.

OLIO SANTO

¼ CUP EXTRA-VIRGIN OLIVE OIL

2 GARLIC CLOVES, CHOPPED

THREE 3-INCH SPRIGS FRESH ROSEMARY

½ TEASPOON CRUSHED HOT RED PEPPER

ONE 11-OUNCE HEAD RADICCHIO

SALT TO TASTE

1 TEASPOON BALSAMIC VINEGAR, PREFER-
ABLY AGED BALSAMICO

1. Build a charcoal fire in an outdoor grill for banked grilling (see page 10) and let burn until the coals are almost completely covered with white ash.

2. To make the *olio santo,* heat the oil, garlic, rosemary, and hot pepper in a small saucepan over low heat until tiny bubbles form around the garlic, about 5 minutes. Remove from the heat and set aside.

3. Cut the radicchio into quarters, leaving the core intact. Brush the radicchio all over to coat lightly with some of the *olio santo* and season with salt.

4. Place the radicchio quarters over the cooler area of the grill and cover. Cook, turning occasionally, until the radicchio is wilted and crisp-tender, about 5 minutes. Transfer to a platter. Drizzle with the remaining *olio santo* and the vinegar and serve hot.

BALSAMIC VINEGAR

True balsamic vinegar is made from sweet Trebbiano grape juice in small batches near Modena, Italy. Long aged in a variety of wooden barrels, it has a deep, complex taste and syrupy texture. Called *balsamico tradizionale,* it is very expensive, but worth the splurge to use, drop by drop, to season foods. It is much too pricey to use for making vinaigrette. Supermarket balsamic vinegar, which is really flavored red wine vinegar, is more than fine for everyday use.

TOMATOES WITH PESTO AND PARMESAN

MAKES 4 SERVINGS
Grilling Method: Indirect High

Is there **an aroma on earth** more enticing than that of fresh basil? These tomatoes are traditionally served alongside steaks and chops as a side dish, but consider making them with another couple of recipes from this chapter as a **vegetarian mixed grill.** Or chop them up and toss them with pasta for a quick sauce, especially in the summer, when tomatoes are at their best.

PESTO

2 GARLIC CLOVES, CRUSHED UNDER A KNIFE AND PEELED

¼ CUP PINE NUTS

½ CUP FRESHLY GRATED PARMESAN OR ROMANO CHEESE

2 CUPS PACKED FRESH BASIL LEAVES

½ CUP EXTRA-VIRGIN OLIVE OIL, AS NEEDED, PLUS MORE FOR STORING

SALT AND FRESHLY GROUND BLACK PEPPER, TO TASTE

2 RIPE MEDIUM TOMATOES

OLIVE OIL, FOR BRUSHING

SALT AND FRESHLY GROUND BLACK PEPPER, TO TASTE

¼ CUP FRESHLY GRATED PARMESAN CHEESE

1. To make the pesto, with the machine running, drop the garlic through the feed tube of a food processor fitted with the metal chopping blade or a blender and process until the garlic is finely chopped. Add the pine nuts and cheese and process until the nuts are finely chopped. Add the basil. With the machine running, add the oil through the tube and process to form a loose paste, adding more oil as needed. Season with salt and pepper. Transfer to a covered container and cover the surface of the pesto with a film of olive oil, which helps keep it from discoloring. (The pesto can be made up to 2 weeks ahead, covered and refrigerated.)

2. Build a charcoal fire in an outdoor grill for indirect high grilling (see page 10) and let burn until the coals are almost completely covered with white ash. (You will not need a drip pan.)

3. Cut each tomato in half through its equator and poke out the seeds with a finger. Brush the tomatoes lightly with olive oil and season lightly with salt and pepper.

4. Lightly oil the grill grate. Place the tomatoes, cut sides up, over the cooler area of the grill and cover. Grill until the tomatoes are heated through and tipped with light brown, about 10 minutes. Spread the top of each tomato with 1 tablespoon of the pesto and sprinkle with 1 tablespoon of cheese. Cover and grill until the cheese melts, about 1½ minutes longer. Transfer to a platter and serve hot.

YUKON GOLD POTATOES WITH LEMON, GARLIC, AND THYME

MAKES 4 TO 6 SERVINGS
Grilling Method: Direct High

Yukon Gold potatoes have thin, edible skins, and you'll save plenty of time prepping them. Par-cooked for quicker grilling, they'll come off the grill **fragrant with garlic and thyme,** tipped with golden brown edges.

⅓ CUP EXTRA-VIRGIN OLIVE OIL

3 TEASPOONS CHOPPED FRESH THYME LEAVES, PREFERABLY LEMON THYME

2 GARLIC CLOVES, CHOPPED

2 POUNDS YUKON GOLD POTATOES, SCRUBBED BUT UNPEELED, CUT INTO 2-INCH CHUNKS

SALT TO TASTE

GRATED ZEST OF 1 LARGE LEMON

FRESHLY GROUND BLACK PEPPER TO TASTE

1. Heat the oil, 2 teaspoons of the thyme, and the garlic in a small saucepan over low heat until tiny bubbles surround the garlic, about 5 minutes. Remove from the heat and set aside.

2. Add enough water to come ½ inch up the sides of a large saucepan and bring to a boil. Place a collapsible steamer in the pot, add the potatoes, and season with salt. Cover tightly and steam the potatoes until they are almost tender when pierced with the tip of a knife, 15 to 20 minutes. Transfer the potatoes to a medium bowl. Add 3 tablespoons of the garlic oil and mix well to lightly coat the potatoes.

3. Build a charcoal fire in an outdoor grill for direct high grilling (see page 8) and let burn until the coals are almost completely covered with white ash.

4. Lightly oil the grill grate. Spread the potatoes in a single layer on the rack and cover. Cook, turning occasionally, until the skins are golden brown, about 5 minutes. Transfer the potatoes to a serving bowl and drizzle with the remaining garlic oil, including the garlic and thyme in the saucepan. Add the lemon zest, sprinkle with the remaining 1 teaspoon of thyme, and season with salt and pepper. Serve hot.

GRILLED PIZZA WITH RATATOUILLE

MAKES 2 TO 4 SERVINGS
Grilling Method: Direct Medium

Grilled pizza showed up on the menu of Al Forno Restaurant in Providence, Rhode Island, about 20 years ago, and it has **spread to every corner** of the country since. Yes, it takes a little dexterity to turn the pizza, but once you get that down, there's no end to the variety of toppings you can use. I sometimes use nothing more than fresh tomatoes and basil with mozzarella. And now that prepared pizza dough is available in supermarkets, homemade pizza can be on your table in no time.

1 POUND FRESH OR THAWED FROZEN PIZZA DOUGH

1 CUP (4 OUNCES) SHREDDED MOZZARELLA CHEESE

1½ CUPS GRILLED RATATOUILLE (PAGE 222)

¾ CUP (3 OUNCES) CRUMBLED RINDLESS GOAT CHEESE (CHÈVRE)

CHOPPED FRESH BASIL, FOR SERVING

CRUSHED HOT RED PEPPER FLAKES, FOR SERVING

1. Build a charcoal fire in an outdoor grill for direct medium grilling (see page 8) and let it burn until the coals are almost completely covered with white ash.

2. Roll out the dough on a very lightly floured work surface into a 12-inch round. If the dough retracts, cover it with plastic wrap, let it rest for 10 minutes, and roll again. Slide the dough onto a well-floured pizza peel or rimless baking sheet. Cover the dough with plastic wrap until ready to grill, up to 20 minutes.

3. Spread the coals in the grill. Let them burn until you can hold your hand over the grill grate for 3 to 4 seconds; this will take about 15 minutes. If the coals are too hot, the dough will burn, so be patient. Lightly oil the grill grate.

4. Slide the pizza onto the grill grate. Cover and grill until the underside of the dough is set and seared with grill marks, about 2 minutes. Using a large metal spatula as an aide, flip the dough over. Sprinkle the pizza with the mozzarella, then dollops of the ratatouille, and finally sprinkle with the goat cheese. Cover again and grill, rotating the dough occasionally to discourage burning from hot spots, until the other side is lightly browned and the dough is cooked through, about 4 minutes. Using the spatula, transfer the pizza back on to the pizza peel or baking sheet.

5. Let stand a few minutes. Sprinkle with the basil and crushed hot pepper, cut into wedges, and serve hot.

GRILLED RATATOUILLE WITH PESTO

MAKES 6 SERVINGS
Grilling Method: Direct High

Classic ratatouille, a pillar of **Provençal cuisine,** is usually a long-simmered ragout of eggplant, bell pepper, zucchini, and tomatoes. But when these same ingredients are grilled and then combined, they retain their individuality while still complementing one another. Don't worry about getting everything off the grill at once, as the vegetables will be reheated anyway. Leftovers make a sensational Grilled Pizza (page 221)—in fact, you may find yourself making the ratatouille so you can make the pizza for another meal.

ONE 1½ POUND EGGPLANT, TRIMMED AND CUT CROSSWISE INTO ½-INCH-THICK ROUNDS

SALT

2 TABLESPOONS EXTRA-VIRGIN OLIVE OIL, PLUS MORE FOR BRUSHING THE VEGETABLES

1 MEDIUM ONION, CHOPPED

2 GARLIC CLOVES, FINELY CHOPPED

3 MEDIUM ZUCCHINI, CUT IN HALF LENGTHWISE

4 LARGE RIPE TOMATOES, CUT IN HALF THROUGH THEIR EQUATORS, SEEDS REMOVED

1 LARGE RED BELL PEPPER, PREPARED FOR GRILLING (SEE "PREPPING GRILLED PEPPERS," PAGE 213)

2 TABLESPOONS PESTO (PAGE 218), OR USE STORE-BOUGHT

¼ TEASPOON CRUSHED HOT RED PEPPER FLAKES

1. Place the eggplant rounds in a large colander and sprinkle all over with about 1½ teaspoons of salt. Let stand to drain off excess bitter juices, about 1 hour. Rinse well and pat dry with paper towels.

2. Meanwhile, heat the oil in a medium saucepan over medium heat. Add the onion and cook, stirring occasionally, until softened, about 5 minutes. Add the garlic and cook until fragrant, about 1 minute. Set the onion mixture aside.

3. Build a charcoal fire in an outdoor grill for direct high grilling (see page 8) and let burn until the coals are almost completely covered with white ash.

4. Brush the eggplant and zucchini all over with oil. The oil should be in a very thin coating, as too much oil will drip onto the coals and cause flare-ups. Lightly oil the grill grate. Place the zucchini and tomatoes, cut sides down, on the grill. Add the bell pepper, skin side down, and eggplant to the grill. Grill the vegetables until done accordingly:

- Red bell pepper: Grill until the skin is charred and blistered, about 10 minutes. Let stand until cool, about 10 minutes. Remove the blackened skin. Coarsely chop into ½-inch dice.

- Eggplant: Grill, turning occasionally, until the eggplant is tender, about 8 minutes. Coarsely chop into ¾-inch dice.

- Tomatoes: Grill until the undersides are seared with grill marks, about 2 minutes. Turn and cook until the skin is charred, about 4 minutes. Discard the skin and coarsely chop the tomatoes into ½-inch dice.

- Zucchini: Grill until the undersides are seared with grill marks, about 3 minutes. Turn and cook until the zucchini is tender, about 5 minutes longer. Coarsely chop into ½-inch dice.

5. Transfer the bell pepper, eggplant, tomatoes, and zucchini to the onion mixture. Bring to a simmer over medium heat, stirring occasionally. Stir in the pesto and crushed red pepper. Season with salt. Serve hot, or cooled to room temperature.

GRILLED VEGETABLE SALAD WITH BASIL VINAIGRETTE

This salad is **an outstanding accompaniment to** many grilled meats, poultry, and fish. It can be made a few hours ahead of serving to avoid last-minute rushing.

¼ CUP EXTRA-VIRGIN OLIVE OIL

2 LARGE GARLIC CLOVES, COARSELY CHOPPED

1 LARGE EAR CORN, UNHUSKED

2 RED BELL PEPPERS, CUT INTO LARGE STRIPS, SEEDS AND CORE REMOVED

2 MEDIUM ZUCCHINI, HALVED LENGTHWISE

4 RIPE PLUM TOMATOES, CUT LENGTHWISE

BASIL VINAIGRETTE

2 TABLESPOONS FRESH LEMON JUICE

1 JALAPEÑO, SEEDED AND MINCED

1 LARGE GARLIC CLOVE, CRUSHED THROUGH A PRESS

⅓ CUP EXTRA-VIRGIN OLIVE OIL

2 TABLESPOONS CHOPPED FRESH BASIL

SALT AND FRESHLY GROUND BLACK PEPPER TO TASTE

1. Build a charcoal fire in an outdoor grill for direct high grilling (see page 8) and let it burn until the coals are almost completely covered with white ash.

2. While the coals are heating, heat the oil and garlic in a small saucepan over medium-low heat until the garlic is golden, about 6 minutes. Set aside.

3. Place the corn and red peppers, skin side down, on the grill. Brush the zucchini and tomatoes with the garlic oil and add to the grill, cut side down. Cover and grill until each vegetable is done accordingly, and transfer to a large platter:

- Corn: Grill, turning occasionally, until the husks are charred, about 20 minutes. Using a clean kitchen towel, remove the husk and silks from the corn. Cut the kernels from the cob.

- Red peppers: Grill until the skin is charred, about 8 minutes. Cool until easy to handle, about 10 minutes. Remove and discard the blackened skin. Cut the peppers into ½-inch dice.

- Zucchini: Cook, turning once, until the zucchini is crisp-tender, about 8 minutes. Cut the zucchini into ¾-inch dice.

- Tomatoes: Grill until the undersides are seared with grill marks, about 2 minutes. Turn and cook until the skin is charred, about 4 minutes. Discard the skin and coarsely chop the tomatoes into ½-inch dice.

4. For the vinaigrette, whisk the lemon juice, jalapeño, and garlic in a large bowl. Gradually whisk in the oil. Add the corn, red peppers, zucchini, tomatoes, and basil and mix well. Season with salt and pepper. Serve warm, or cooled to room temperature.

DESSERTS

SPICY MEXICAN BROWNIES

MAKES 9 SERVINGS

Grilling Method: Indirect Medium

At first glance, you might think that chiles in your brownies are weird, but have an open mind and give these a try. We're talking about sweet ancho chiles here, not killer-hot chipotles, and they harmonize *perfectamente* with the **cinnamon and almonds,** as well as any smoky flavors from the grill. If you aren't convinced, leave them out and you'll still have great brownies. Lining the pan with foil as directed makes it easy to lift out the entire batch, so you don't have to dig them out of the pan.

SOFTENED BUTTER AND FLOUR, FOR THE PAN

8 TABLESPOONS (1 STICK) UNSALTED BUTTER, CUT UP

5 OUNCES SEMISWEET CHOCOLATE, COARSELY CHOPPED

1 CUP PACKED LIGHT BROWN SUGAR

2 LARGE EGGS, AT ROOM TEMPERATURE

1 TEASPOON VANILLA EXTRACT

1 CUP ALL-PURPOSE FLOUR

1/2 CUP SLICED NATURAL ALMONDS

2 TEASPOONS GROUND ANCHO CHILES

1/2 TEASPOON GROUND CINNAMON

1/4 TEASPOON BAKING SODA

1/4 TEASPOON SALT

1. Build a charcoal fire in an outdoor grill for indirect medium grilling (see page 9) and let burn until the coals are almost completely covered with white ash. You will not need a drip pan.

2. Butter an 8-inch square metal baking pan. Line the bottom and 2 sides of the pan with an 18-inch-long strip of aluminum foil, folding the foil lengthwise to fit into the pan. Leave the foil overhanging the sides to act as handles. Butter the pan and foil, dust with flour, and tap out the excess flour.

3. Melt the butter in a medium saucepan over medium heat. Remove from the heat and add the chocolate. Let stand until the chocolate melts, then whisk until smooth. Whisk in the brown sugar. Whisk in the eggs, one at a time, then the vanilla.

4. Process the flour and almonds in a food processor fitted with the metal blade until the almonds are ground into a powder. Add the ground chiles, cinnamon, baking soda, and salt and pulse to combine. Add to the saucepan and stir with a spoon until combined. Scrape into the baking pan and smooth the top.

5. Adjust the vents on the grill to maintain a temperature of 350° to 400°F. Place the pan over the empty part of the grill and cover. Grill until a toothpick inserted in the center of the brownie comes out with a moist crumb, about 30 minutes. Do not overbake.

6. Place the pan on a wire cake rack and cool completely. Run a knife around the inside of the pan and lift up on the handles to remove the brownie from the pan. Cut into 9 equal pieces. (The brownies can be stored in an airtight container at room temperature for up to 3 days.)

CHERRY CLAFOUTI

MAKES 8 SERVINGS
Grilling Method: Indirect Medium

Clafouti (kla-foo-TEE) is a hybrid of a **rustic French dessert,** somewhat of a cross between a fruit-studded custard and a creamy cake. It can be made with other fruits, such as thinly sliced peaches, pears, or plums, but it is best known for this cherry version—if you live near a source for **sour cherries,** use them, knowing that sweet cherries are very good, too. In France, most cooks believe that clafoutis should be made with unpitted cherries, something that probably won't go over big at an American cookout.

3 TABLESPOONS UNSALTED BUTTER, CUT UP

2 TABLESPOONS PLUS ½ CUP SUGAR

1½ CUPS HALF-AND-HALF

4 LARGE EGGS, AT ROOM TEMPERATURE

2 TABLESPOONS KIRSCH (CLEAR CHERRY EAU-DE-VIE), CHERRY BRANDY, OR BRANDY

1 TEASPOON VANILLA EXTRACT

1¼ CUPS ALL-PURPOSE FLOUR

¼ TEASPOON SALT

1½ CUPS PITTED FRESH SOUR OR BING CHERRIES, OR USE FROZEN OR DRAINED CANNED SOUR CHERRIES

CONFECTIONERS' SUGAR, FOR SERVING

1. Build a charcoal fire in an outdoor grill for indirect medium grilling (see page 9) and let burn until the coals are almost completely covered with white ash. You will not need a drip pan.

2. Melt the butter in a small saucepan over medium heat. Brush the inside of a 9-inch-diameter metal cake pan with 1½-inch sides with some of the butter. Set the remaining butter aside. Sprinkle with 2 tablespoons of the sugar, tilt to coat the inside of the pan with sugar, and tap out the excess.

3. Combine the half-and-half, reserved melted butter, eggs, kirsch, and vanilla in a blender. Add the flour, the remaining ½ cup of sugar, and salt and process, stopping occasionally to scrape down the sides of the blender jar, until smooth. Scatter the cherries evenly in the pan and add the batter.

4. Adjust the vents on the grill to maintain a temperature of 350° to 400°F. Place the pan over the empty part of the grill and cover. Grill until the clafouti feels set when pressed in the center and the edges are puffed and pull away from the sides of the pan, 50 to 60 minutes.

5. Place the pan on a wire cake rack and cool until warm or to room temperature. Sift confectioners' sugar generously over the top. Cut into wedges and serve.

DESSERTS ON THE GRILL

Serve your guests a delicious dessert at the end of the meal, and you will literally have them eating out of your hand. But when you inform them that it was cooked on the grill, they are likely to be surprised, too. Even the most accomplished grilling fan tends to overlook their favorite cooking method when it comes to sweets. Too bad, because the results are surprisingly excellent—and you don't have to turn on the oven during the hot weather, either. The truth is, just about anything that you can bake, you can grill. But there are a few tips:

- Use old-fashioned recipes for baked goods that aren't particularly fussy about exact temperatures. Cobblers, crisps, brownies, and other goodies are more forgiving with fluctuating temperatures than a cake.

- Choose the ripest, juiciest fruit at the market for your grilled desserts. All of the sugar and spices in the world won't boost the taste of dull, under-ripe fruit.

- When grilling fruit on the grill, be sure to scrub the grate well to remove any residual flavors. If you have used wood chips, and some smoke is lingering, choose a recipe with spices that will actually be complemented by the smokiness. For example, a hint of mesquite flavor with the Spicy Mexican Brownies (page 228) is quite welcome.

- A cast-iron skillet is a very versatile utensil in general, but it is great for grilled desserts. Just be sure never to wash it in soap and water, or you will remove its seasoning. To clean, scrub out the skillet with hot water and a plastic scrubber or brush. Add a handful of salt and scrub it again, using the salt as an abrasive. Rinse out the skillet, dry with a towel, and heat it over high heat to evaporate excess water and to sterilize it. Let cool, then store.

BLUEBERRY BUCKLE

MAKES 8 SERVINGS

Grilling Method: Indirect Medium

Buckles, along with grunts, cobblers, and pandowdies, belong to the family of American fruit desserts with improbable names. However, when you consider that a buckle does have a bumpy top, its name makes more sense than most. Your friends will not believe that this **old-fashioned treat,** bursting with **berries** and crowned with lots of **streusel,** came from the grill.

STREUSEL

⅓ CUP PLUS 1 TABLESPOON ALL-PURPOSE FLOUR

¼ CUP PACKED LIGHT BROWN SUGAR

½ TEASPOON GROUND CINNAMON

4 TABLESPOONS (½ STICK) UNSALTED BUTTER, AT ROOM TEMPERATURE

SOFTENED BUTTER AND FLOUR, FOR THE PAN

1½ CUPS ALL-PURPOSE FLOUR

¾ CUP GRANULATED SUGAR

2 TEASPOONS BAKING POWDER

½ TEASPOON SALT

½ CUP WHOLE MILK

2 LARGE EGGS, AT ROOM TEMPERATURE

4 TABLESPOONS (½ STICK) UNSALTED BUTTER, WELL SOFTENED

2 CUPS FRESH OR FROZEN BLUEBERRIES

1. Build a charcoal fire in an outdoor grill for indirect medium grilling (see page 9) and let burn until the coals are almost completely covered with white ash. You will not need a drip pan.

2. To make the streusel, combine the flour, brown sugar, and cinnamon in a small bowl. Add the butter and rub with your fingers until crumbly. Set aside.

3. Butter and flour the inside of a 9-inch-diameter metal cake pan with 1½-inch sides and tap out the excess flour. Whisk the flour, granulated sugar, baking powder, and salt in a medium bowl to combine. Add the milk, eggs, and softened butter. Mix with an electric hand-held mixer on low speed to moisten. Increase the speed to high and mix, scraping down the sides of the bowl with a rubber spatula as needed, until smooth and fluffy, about 2 minutes. Two tips here: The butter must be well softened to integrate into the batter, and use a timer for the 2-minute mixing period, as it takes that long to incorporate the right amount of air into the batter. Fold in the berries. Spread the batter evenly in the pan. Sprinkle evenly with the streusel.

4. Adjust the vents on the grill to maintain a temperature of 350° to 400°F. Place the pan over the empty part of the grill and cover. Grill until a toothpick inserted in the center of the buckle comes out clean and the edges pull away from the sides of the pan, 50 to 60 minutes.

5. Place the pan on a wire cake rack and cool. Cut into wedges and serve warm or cooled to room temperature. (The buckle can be made, covered with plastic wrap and stored at room temperature, up to 2 days ahead.)

PEACH GRANOLA CRISP

The arrival of ripe peaches coincides with the height of the barbecue season. Here's a great recipe for a **favorite summertime dessert,** peach crisp. As a time-saver, the topping is made with your favorite granola—just be sure to choose a flavor that won't compete with the peaches. You'll need a cast-iron skillet for this dessert.

6 CUPS (ABOUT 7) RIPE MEDIUM PEACHES, PEELED AND SLICED (SEE NOTE)

½ CUP PACKED LIGHT BROWN SUGAR

2 TABLESPOONS CORNSTARCH

2 CUPS GRANOLA

3 TABLESPOONS UNSALTED BUTTER, MELTED

VANILLA ICE CREAM, FOR SERVING

1. Build a charcoal fire in an outdoor grill for indirect medium grilling (see page 9) and let burn until the coals are almost completely covered with white ash. You will not need a drip pan.

2. Mix the peaches, brown sugar, and cornstarch together in a medium bowl. Scrape into a 9- to 10-inch cast-iron skillet. Mix the granola and melted butter together in a small bowl and set aside.

3. Adjust the vents on the grill to maintain a temperature of 350° to 400°F. Place the skillet over the coals and cover. Grill, stirring occasionally, until the peach juices bubble. Move the skillet to the empty area of the grill. Sprinkle evenly with the granola mixture. Grill until the peach juices have thickened and the granola topping is crisp, about 10 minutes. Serve warm, or cooled to room temperature, with the ice cream.

Note: To peel peaches, first be sure that the peaches are ripe. If they are firm and under-ripe, the skin will be difficult to remove. Bring a large saucepan of water to a boil over high heat. A few at a time, add the peaches to the water and cook until the skin loosens, about 1 minute. Use a slotted spoon to transfer the peaches to a large bowl of ice water. Use a small sharp knife to remove the skins.

SUMMER BERRY COBBLER

MAKES 4 SERVINGS
Grilling Method: Indirect Medium

Here's another favorite summertime treat that you can toss together in a **cast-iron skillet** and bake up on the grill. Use your **favorite berries,** with one caveat—don't use all strawberries, as they tend to lose their color when heated. Tapioca is a better choice than cornstarch to thicken the juices here, as the acidity of some berries can weaken the thickening powder of the latter.

BERRIES

6 CUPS MIXED BERRIES, SUCH AS BLUEBERRIES, BLACKBERRIES, RASPBERRIES, AND SLICED STRAWBERRIES

2/3 CUP SUGAR

2 TABLESPOONS INSTANT TAPIOCA, GROUND IN A BLENDER UNTIL PULVERIZED, OR USE TAPIOCA FLOUR

3 TABLESPOONS UNSALTED BUTTER, CUT UP

TOPPING

1 CUP ALL-PURPOSE FLOUR

2 TABLESPOONS SUGAR

1 TEASPOON BAKING POWDER

1/4 TEASPOON SALT

1/4 CUP WHOLE MILK

1 LARGE EGG YOLK

1/2 TEASPOON VANILLA EXTRACT

VANILLA ICE CREAM, FOR SERVING

1. Build a charcoal fire in an outdoor grill for indirect medium grilling (see page 9) and let burn until the coals are almost completely covered with white ash. You will not need a drip pan.

2. To prepare the berries, mix the berries, sugar, and tapioca in a medium bowl. Add the butter. Spread evenly in a 9- to 10-inch-diameter cast-iron skillet.

3. To prepare the topping, whisk the flour, sugar, baking powder, and salt in a medium bowl to combine. Whisk the milk, yolk, and vanilla in another bowl to combine. Pour into the flour mixture and stir with a wooden spoon to form a soft dough. Divide the dough into 4 equal portions. One at a time, pat the dough in your hands to form a biscuit about 3 inches in diameter. Place the biscuits on top of the berries.

4. Adjust the vents on the grill to maintain a temperature of 350° to 400°F. Place the skillet in the empty portion of the grill and cover. Grill until the berry juices are bubbling throughout and a toothpick inserted in a biscuit comes out clean, about 30 minutes. Serve hot or warm with ice cream.

PINEAPPLE-GINGER UPSIDE DOWN CAKE

MAKES 6 TO 8 SERVINGS
Grilling Method: Indirect Medium

This is the perfect example of an old-fashioned recipe that not only can be cooked on a grill, but **updates beautifully** for today's tastes, as well. Fresh pineapple, crystallized ginger, and a firmer cake much improve the canned-fruit standby. One element remains constant—a cast-iron skillet is needed to cook the **caramel-like topping.**

TOPPING

1 CUP PACKED LIGHT OR DARK BROWN SUGAR

6 TABLESPOONS (¾ STICK) UNSALTED BUTTER, CUT UP

FOUR ½-INCH-THICK SLICES RIPE FRESH PINEAPPLE, CORED, CUT IN HALF CROSSWISE TO MAKE 8 PIECES TOTAL

⅓ CUP CHOPPED CRYSTALLIZED GINGER

1½ CUPS ALL-PURPOSE FLOUR

1 CUP SUGAR

1½ TEASPOONS BAKING POWDER

¼ TEASPOON SALT

8 TABLESPOONS (1 STICK) UNSALTED BUTTER, WELL SOFTENED

½ CUP WHOLE MILK

2 LARGE EGGS, AT ROOM TEMPERATURE

1 TEASPOON VANILLA EXTRACT

1. Build a charcoal fire in an outdoor grill for indirect medium grilling (see page 9) and let burn until the coals are almost completely covered with white ash. You will not need a drip pan.

2. To make the topping, mix the brown sugar and butter in a 9- to 10-inch-diameter cast-iron skillet. Place the skillet over the coals. Cook, whisking often, until the brown sugar is melted and smooth, about 3 minutes. Remove from the heat. Place the pineapple slices in a spoke pattern in the brown sugar mixture, and sprinkle with the ginger. Set aside. Cover the grill while making the cake batter.

3. Whisk the flour, sugar, baking powder, and salt in a medium bowl. Add the butter, milk, eggs, and vanilla. Mix with a hand-held electric mixer on low speed to moisten. Increase the speed to high and mix, scraping down the sides of the bowl with a rubber spatula as needed, for 2 minutes, until smooth and fluffy. Two tips here: The butter must be well softened to integrate into the batter, and use a timer for the 2-minute mixing period, as it takes that long to incorporate the right amount of air into the batter. Scrape into the skillet and smooth the top.

4. Adjust the vents on the grill to maintain a temperature of 350° to 400°F. Place the skillet over the empty area of the grill. Grill until the cake is lightly browned and a toothpick inserted in the center of the cake comes out clean, about 25 minutes.

5. Cool the cake for 5 to 10 minutes. Run a knife around the inside of the skillet. Place a rimmed round platter over the skillet. Holding the platter and skillet together, quickly invert to unmold the cake. Cool completely.

GRILLED FIGS WITH MASCARPONE AND HONEY

MAKES 6 SERVINGS
Grilling Method: Direct Medium

When figs make their **late-summer** appearance, grill them to draw even more of their honeyed sweetness to the fore. Adjust the grilling time according to the size of the figs, which can range from quite small to relatively hefty. Their lushness is balanced with **creamy mascarpone,** the "secret ingredient" in tiramisù, and their nectar played up with a **drizzle of honey.** This dessert looks sensational in parfait glasses or small dessert bowls, and you might want to serve Italian cookies alongside. And so you won't have to turn each fig, you may want to use a grilling basket. If you don't want to use mascarpone, substitute ½ cup heavy cream, whipped.

24 RIPE SMALL FIGS OR 12 TO 16 LARGE FIGS

VEGETABLE OIL, FOR BRUSHING

8 OUNCES MASCARPONE

½ CUP FULL-FLAVORED HONEY

⅓ CUP SLICED NATURAL ALMONDS, TOASTED (SEE "TOASTING NUTS," PAGE 244)

1. Build a charcoal fire in an outdoor grill for direct medium grilling (see page 8) and let burn until the coals are almost completely covered with white ash.

2. Trim the figs and cut large figs in half lengthwise. Brush them lightly with the oil. If you wish, place them in a lightly oiled grilling basket and clip the basket closed.

3. Place the figs over the coals on the grill and cover. Grill, turning the figs (or basket) once, until they are lightly browned and give off bubbling juices, about 5 minutes.

4. For each serving, place 2 figs in a parfait glass or dessert bowl. Top with a dollop of mascarpone, and about 1½ teaspoons honey. Add 2 more figs, another dollop mascarpone, and 1½ teaspoons honey. Sprinkle each with toasted almonds. Serve immediately.

PINEAPPLE KEBABS WITH RASPBERRY SAUCE

MAKES 4 SERVINGS
Grilling Method: Direct High

Pick up a peeled pineapple at the supermarket, and you are on your way to one of the **freshest, easiest, and tastiest desserts** you can serve from the grill—chunks of grilled pineapple with a **vibrant red raspberry sauce** look great, too. If you want a lighter dessert, leave out the ice cream or use sorbet, and it will still get raves from guests. Skewering the pineapple chunks makes them easier to grill, but don't feel that you have to serve them that way.

RASPBERRY SAUCE

2 CUPS FRESH RASPBERRIES

2 TABLESPOONS SUGAR, PREFERABLY SUPERFINE, OR MORE TO TASTE

1 TABLESPOON FRESH LEMON JUICE

1 RIPE PINEAPPLE, PEELED AND CORED

VEGETABLE OIL, FOR BRUSHING

VANILLA ICE CREAM, FOR SERVING

1. To make the raspberry sauce, process the raspberries, sugar, and lemon juice in a food processor or blender until smooth. Taste and adjust the sweetness with more sugar, if needed. Strain through a fine wire mesh strainer into a bowl. Cover and refrigerate until chilled, at least 2 hours. (The sauce can be made 2 days ahead.)

2. Build a charcoal fire in an outdoor grill for direct high grilling (see page 8) and let burn until the coals are almost completely covered with white ash.

3. Cut the pineapple into 1-inch-thick slices. Cut each slice into 6 wedges. Thread 6 wedges onto each of 4 metal skewers. Lightly brush the pineapple with oil.

4. Place the skewers on the grill and cover. Grill until the undersides are seared with grill marks, about 2 minutes. Turn, cover, and grill until the other sides are seared and the pineapple is heated through, about 2 minutes longer. Slide the pineapple off the skewers onto a plate.

5. Divide the pineapple among 4 dessert bowls. Top with a scoop of ice cream, then the raspberry sauce. Serve immediately.

BANANA SUNDAES WITH AMARETTO BUTTERSCOTCH SAUCE

MAKES 6 SERVINGS
Grilling Method: Banked

Wrapped in individual foil packets, these grilled bananas make their own **gooey, buttery sauce** to pour over a bowl of vanilla ice cream (if you find toasted pecan, so much the better). Almond-flavored liqueur makes this a dessert for grownups, so if kids are part of the party, substitute apple juice for the liqueur, or make theirs separately, identifying their packets with a marker. Another time, substitute ripe peaches, peeled and cut into wedges, for the bananas.

6 RIPE BANANAS, PEELED

¾ CUP PACKED LIGHT BROWN SUGAR

12 TABLESPOONS (1½ STICKS) UNSALTED BUTTER, CUT INTO 12 PATS

¾ CUP ALMOND-FLAVORED LIQUEUR, SUCH AS AMARETTO DI SARONNO

VANILLA ICE CREAM, FOR SERVING

1. Tear off six 12-inch-square pieces of heavy-duty aluminum foil and fold in half. For each dessert, cut a banana into ½-inch rounds and place in the center of the bottom half of the foil. Top with 2 tablespoons brown sugar and 2 tablespoons butter. Pour 2 tablespoons liqueur over the sugar. (The sugar will absorb some of the liqueur and keep it from running off the foil.) Fold the foil over and crimp the 3 open sides tightly closed. (The packets can be prepared up to 4 hours ahead, stored at room temperature.)

2. Build a charcoal fire in an outdoor grill for banked grilling (see page 10) and let burn until the coals are almost completely covered with white ash.

3. Place the foil packets on the cooler area of the grill and cover. Grill, without turning, until the butter, sugar, and liqueur have melted together into a sauce (snip open a packet with scissors to check), about 8 minutes.

4. Scoop the ice cream into 6 dessert bowls. Cut open each packet with scissors and pour the contents over the ice cream. Serve immediately.

GRILLED NECTARINES WITH LIME-GINGER BUTTER

MAKES 6 SERVINGS
Grilling Method: Banked

This dessert may seem a bit austere, but when nectarines are **ripe, juicy, and flavorful,** there are few ways that show them off to such advantage. Make the butter ahead of time so it will be soft, fluffy, and quick to melt over the hot stone fruit.

LIME-GINGER BUTTER

ONE 4-INCH LENGTH FRESH GINGER, PEELED AND SHREDDED ON THE LARGE HOLES OF A BOX GRATER

8 TABLESPOONS (1 STICK) UNSALTED BUTTER, SOFTENED

GRATED ZEST OF 1 LIME

6 LARGE RIPE NECTARINES

VEGETABLE OIL, FOR BRUSHING

1. In batches, squeeze the ginger in your fist over a small bowl to extract the juice. You should have 2 tablespoons ginger juice. Add the butter and lime zest and mix with a rubber spatula until combined. Set aside.

2. Build a charcoal fire in an outdoor grill for banked grilling (see page 10) and let burn until the coals are almost completely covered with white ash.

3. Cut the nectarines in half and remove the pits. Brush the nectarines lightly with oil. Lightly oil the grill grate. Place the nectarines on the hotter area of the grill, cut sides down, and cover. Grill until the undersides are seared with grill marks, about 2 minutes. Using a long-handled metal spatula (tongs may squash the fruit), turn the nectarines and move them to the cooler area of the grill, cut sides up. Cover and grill until the skins are split and the nectarines are heated through, about 5 minutes.

4. Bring a tray with 6 dessert bowls to the grill. Transfer 2 nectarine halves to each of the bowls. Top each serving with equal amounts of the butter and serve at once.

TOASTING NUTS

The heat of the oven browns the surface of nuts, deepening their flavor and crisping them, too. Some cooks like toasting the nuts in a skillet, but this works well only for small, round pine nuts. Most other nuts should be baked. Don't feel that you need to heat up your range for this easy task, especially in warm summer weather. It is much easier to use a toaster oven, especially when you are toasting ½ cup or fewer nuts.

Preheat the oven (or toaster oven) to 350°F. Spread the nuts in a baking sheet (or the toaster tray). Bake, occasionally stirring the nuts, until they are lightly toasted and fragrant, about 10 minutes. Transfer to a plate to cool.

TOP TWELVE COOKOUT SIDE DISHES

CREAMY POTATO SALAD

MAKES 8 TO 12 SERVINGS

What is a **backyard cookout** without potato salad? There is an ongoing argument over which potato is best for salad—fluffy, dry boiling potatoes or firm, waxy boiling potatoes. Use Yukon Golds, which have qualities of both varieties, plus **a nice buttery flavor,** and do not require peeling.

3½ POUNDS YUKON GOLD POTATOES

3 TABLESPOONS CIDER VINEGAR

¾ CUP MAYONNAISE

¾ CUP SOUR CREAM

1½ TABLESPOONS YELLOW PREPARED OR DIJON MUSTARD

⅓ CUP SWEET PICKLE RELISH

4 HARD-BOILED EGGS, SLICED

4 CELERY RIBS WITH LEAVES, CHOPPED

4 SCALLIONS, WHITE AND GREEN PARTS, CHOPPED

3 TABLESPOONS CHOPPED FRESH PARSLEY, PLUS MORE FOR GARNISH

SALT AND FRESHLY GROUND BLACK PEPPER TO TASTE

1. Scrub the potatoes under cold running water. Place them in a large pot and add enough cold salted water to cover the potatoes. Cover with a lid and bring to a boil over high heat. Reduce the heat to medium and keep the lid ajar. Cook until the potatoes are tender when pierced with the tip of a small knife, about 25 minutes. Drain and rinse under cold water until cool enough to handle but still warm.

2. If desired, peel the potatoes. Slice the potatoes into ½-inch-thick rounds and place in a large bowl. Sprinkle the warm potatoes with the vinegar. Cool.

3. Whisk the mayonnaise, sour cream, mustard, and relish in a medium bowl. Add to the potatoes. Add the eggs, celery, scallions, and parsley, and mix. Season with salt and pepper. Cover and refrigerate until chilled, at least 2 hours. (The salad can be made up to 1 day ahead, covered and refrigerated.) Sprinkle with additional parsley to garnish, and serve chilled.

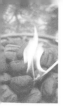

CLASSIC COLESLAW

Most store-bought coleslaws are too sweet—this one is **just right.** (If you have a sweet tooth where coleslaw is concerned, just add more sugar.) If you wish, to save time and effort, substitute 3 pounds of precut coleslaw mix (sold in the produce aisle) for the freshly cut **cabbage and carrots.**

1 SMALL (2½ POUNDS) GREEN CABBAGE

3 MEDIUM CARROTS, SHREDDED

3 SCALLIONS, WHITE AND GREEN PARTS, CHOPPED

1⅓ CUPS MAYONNAISE

3 TABLESPOONS CIDER VINEGAR

2 TABLESPOONS SUGAR

1 TEASPOON CELERY SEEDS

SALT AND FRESHLY GROUND BLACK PEPPER TO TASTE

1. Cut the cabbage into quarters and remove the core. Cut the quarters to fit the feed tube of a food processor fitted with the metal slicing blade. Process the cabbage to slice it. (You can also use a large knife to shred the cabbage.) Transfer to a large bowl. Add the carrots and scallions, and mix.

2. Whisk the mayonnaise, vinegar, sugar, and celery seeds together in a small bowl. Pour over the slaw and mix well. Season with salt and pepper. Cover and refrigerate until chilled, at least 2 hours. (The slaw can be made up to 2 days ahead, covered and refrigerated.) Serve chilled.

ITALIAN MACARONI SALAD

This **hearty side salad** is a cross between the old-fashioned macaroni salad and the newer darling of the deli counter, pasta salad. Add other embellishments as you see fit—marinated artichoke hearts, chopped salami, or cubes of provolone cheese.

8 OUNCES DITALINI OR OTHER SHORT TUBULAR PASTA

2 TABLESPOONS RED WINE VINEGAR

¾ CUP MAYONNAISE

3 CELERY RIBS, CHOPPED

1 LARGE GRILL-ROASTED RED BELL PEPPER (SEE PAGE 212), CHOPPED

½ CUP CHOPPED PITTED KALAMATA OLIVES

⅓ CUP CHOPPED RED ONION

¼ CUP CHOPPED FRESH BASIL

SALT AND FRESHLY GROUND BLACK PEPPER TO TASTE

1. Bring a large pot of lightly salted water to a boil over high heat. Add the pasta and cook until tender, about 8 minutes. Drain and rinse under cold running water until cool. Drain well. Transfer to a large bowl.

2. Sprinkle the pasta with the vinegar. Add the mayonnaise, celery, red pepper, olives, red onion, and basil, and mix. Season with salt and pepper. Cover and refrigerate until chilled, at least 2 hours. (The salad can be made up to 2 days ahead, covered and refrigerated.) Serve chilled.

LAYERED GREEN SALAD WITH RANCH DRESSING

MAKES 8 SERVINGS

Green salad can be a problem to transport to a cookout because most vinaigrette dressings wilt the lettuce. Due to **clever layering** of the ingredients and delicious, **thick ranch dressing,** this salad can be made up to 24 hours before serving. Be sure that you have a bowl large enough to contain and toss the salad.

8 CUPS COARSELY CHOPPED ICEBERG LETTUCE (ABOUT ⅔ OF AN AVERAGE HEAD)

1 PINT GRAPE OR CHERRY TOMATOES

2 CUPS BROCCOLI FLORETS, COOKED UNTIL CRISP-TENDER

2 CUPS THAWED FROZEN PEAS

8 OUNCES WHITE MUSHROOMS, SLICED

1 CUP MAYONNAISE

1 CUP SOUR CREAM

ONE 1-OUNCE PACKAGE HIDDEN VALLEY RANCH® SALAD DRESSING AND SEASONING MIX

2 CUPS (8 OUNCES) SHREDDED CHEDDAR CHEESE

6 BACON STRIPS, COOKED UNTIL CRISP, CRUMBLED

1. Place the lettuce in a 4½-quart bowl. Top with, in the following order, the tomatoes, broccoli, peas, and mushrooms.

2. Combine the mayonnaise, sour cream, and seasoning mix in a small bowl. Spoon over the vegetables and smooth the dressing with a rubber spatula to completely cover the vegetables. Sprinkle with the cheese, then the bacon. Cover and refrigerate until chilled, at least 2 hours. (The salad can be made up to 1 day ahead, covered and refrigerated.)

3. To serve, toss well to combine the vegetables and dressing, and serve immediately.

FOUR-BEAN SALAD WITH SWEET ONION DRESSING

A **colorful, marinated** mix of fresh and prepared beans in a sweet onion dressing—it doesn't get much more down home and delicious than that.

SWEET ONION DRESSING

¾ CUP PLUS 1 TABLESPOON VEGETABLE OIL

1 MEDIUM SWEET ONION, SUCH AS VIDALIA, CHOPPED

¼ CUP CIDER VINEGAR

1 TEASPOON SUGAR

SALT AND FRESHLY GROUND BLACK PEPPER TO TASTE

12 OUNCES GREEN BEANS, TRIMMED AND CUT INTO 1-INCH LENGTHS

ONE 19-OUNCE CAN GARBANZO BEANS (CHICKPEAS), DRAINED AND RINSED

ONE 19-OUNCE CAN DARK KIDNEY BEANS, DRAINED AND RINSED

ONE 19-OUNCE CAN PINK BEANS, DRAINED AND RINSED

1. To make the dressing, heat 1 tablespoon of the oil in a medium skillet over medium heat. Add the onion and cover. Cook, stirring occasionally, until the onion is tender, about 10 minutes. Transfer to a blender and add the remaining ¾ cup of oil, the vinegar, sugar, salt, and pepper and blend until the dressing is thickened and the onions are finely chopped, but not puréed.

2. Bring a large saucepan of lightly salted water to a boil over high heat. Add the green beans and cook until crisp-tender, about 3 minutes. Drain and rinse under cold running water. Pat the green beans dry with paper towels. Transfer the green beans to a large bowl.

3. Add the garbanzo, red kidney, and pink beans to the bowl. Add the onion dressing and mix well. Season again with salt and pepper. Cover and refrigerate until chilled, at least 2 hours. (The salad can be made up to 1 day ahead, covered and refrigerated.) Serve chilled.

OUTRAGEOUS MACARONI AND CHEESE

Macaroni and cheese, at least in this **three-cheese incarnation,** is one of those side dishes that can really sneak up on you—if you aren't careful, you will have eaten your fill of it before you even get to the main course. **For extra kick,** use pepper Jack cheese instead of Monterey Jack. If you wish, cook the mac' n' cheese in the grill with indirect medium heat for about 25 minutes.

1 POUND ELBOW MACARONI

6 TABLESPOONS UNSALTED BUTTER

⅓ CUP ALL-PURPOSE FLOUR

3 CUPS WHOLE MILK, HEATED (IN A MICROWAVE OVEN OR ON THE STOVE)

2 CUPS (8 OUNCES) SHREDDED SHARP CHEDDAR CHEESE

2 CUPS (8 OUNCES) SHREDDED MONTEREY JACK

HOT RED PEPPER SAUCE, TO TASTE

¼ CUP FRESHLY GRATED PARMESAN CHEESE

2 TABLESPOONS DRIED BREAD CRUMBS

1. Position a rack in the center of the oven and preheat to 350°F. Butter a 2½-quart baking dish.

2. Bring a large saucepan of lightly salted water to a boil over high heat. Add the macaroni and cook until it is almost, but not quite, tender, about 8 minutes. Drain well and set aside.

3. Melt 5 tablespoons of butter in the same saucepan over medium-low heat. Add the flour, whisk until smooth, and let bubble without browning for about 1 minute. Whisk in the hot milk, increase the heat to high, and bring to a boil, whisking often. Reduce the heat to low, whisk in the cheddar and Monterey Jack cheeses, and cook until the cheese is melted. Season with hot pepper sauce. Add the pasta and mix well. Transfer to the baking dish.

4. Mix the Parmesan cheese and bread crumbs together in a small bowl and sprinkle over the macaroni. Dot with the remaining 1 tablespoon of butter. Bake until the topping is browned and the sauce is bubbling, about 25 minutes. Serve hot.

GINGERED BAKED BEANS

Grilled franks can look pretty plain until you **spoon up some baked beans** to serve alongside. Thanks to a can of **ginger ale** stirred into the pot, which adds sugar and spice, these will be among the best beans you've ever had.

4 BACON STRIPS, COARSELY CHOPPED

1 LARGE ONION, CHOPPED

TWO 19-OUNCE CANS CANNELLINI (WHITE KIDNEY) BEANS, RINSED AND DRAINED

TWO 19-OUNCE CANS PINK BEANS, RINSED AND DRAINED

ONE 12-OUNCE CAN GINGER ALE (NOT DIET)

1 CUP TOMATO KETCHUP

1/3 CUP SPICY BROWN MUSTARD

1. Position a rack in the center of the oven and preheat to 350°F.

2. Cook the bacon in a Dutch oven or flameproof casserole over medium heat, stirring often, until it begins to brown, about 5 minutes. Add the onion and cook, stirring often, until the onion is golden brown, about 8 minutes. Stir in the cannellini and pink beans, ginger ale, ketchup, and mustard and bring to a simmer. Cover tightly.

3. Transfer to the oven and bake for 45 minutes. Uncover and bake until the sauce has thickened, about 15 minutes. Serve hot.

NOT-TOO-SWEET CORNBREAD

Is there a quick bread that is any easier or tastier than cornbread? Good bakers keep a container of **buttermilk** in the refrigerator for recipes like this, knowing that the acids in the buttermilk make for **very tender baked goods.** A combination of yogurt and milk is an acceptable substitution.

4 TABLESPOONS UNSALTED BUTTER, MELTED, AND DIVIDED

⅔ CUP YELLOW CORNMEAL, PREFERABLY STONE-GROUND

⅔ CUP ALL-PURPOSE FLOUR

1 TABLESPOON SUGAR

½ TEASPOON BAKING SODA

½ TEASPOON SALT

1 CUP BUTTERMILK, OR ¾ CUP PLAIN YOGURT WHISKED WITH ¼ CUP WHOLE MILK

1 LARGE EGG, BEATEN

1. Position a rack in the center of the oven and preheat to 400°F. Pour 2 tablespoons of melted butter into an 8-inch square baking pan. Place the pan in the oven until it is very hot, about 2 minutes. Don't worry if the butter browns a bit.

2. Whisk the cornmeal, flour, sugar, baking soda, and salt in a medium bowl to combine. Make a well in the center. Whisk the buttermilk, egg, and remaining 2 tablespoons melted butter in another medium bowl. Pour the wet ingredients into the well in the dry ingredients and mix with a wooden spoon just until the batter is smooth—do not overmix. Spread evenly in the hot pan.

3. Bake until the top is golden brown and springs back when pressed in the center, about 20 minutes.

4. Cool in the pan for 5 minutes. Cut into squares and serve hot.

VARIATION

Spicy Cheese Cornbread: Add ½ cup shredded extra-sharp cheddar cheese and 1 jalapeño, seeded and minced, to the batter. Sprinkle ⅓ cup shredded extra-sharp cheddar cheese on the batter just before baking.

BUTTERMILK BISCUITS

For the most tender, **melt-in-your-mouth biscuits,** you can't beat the combination of buttermilk and vegetable shortening. No need to use butter in the biscuit dough, as you will probably slather your biscuit with plenty of butter anyway.

2 CUPS ALL-PURPOSE FLOUR

1½ TEASPOONS BAKING POWDER

½ TEASPOON BAKING SODA

½ TEASPOON SALT

½ CUP "NO TRANS FAT" VEGETABLE SHORTENING, CHILLED, CUT INTO THIN SLICES

1 CUP BUTTERMILK, OR ¾ CUP PLAIN YOGURT WHISKED WITH ¼ CUP WHOLE MILK

1. Position a rack in the center of the oven and preheat to 400°F.

2. Whisk the flour, baking powder, baking soda, and salt in a medium bowl to combine. Add the shortening and cut in with a pastry blender (or use two knives in a crossing pattern) until the mixture resembles coarse cornmeal. Make a well in the center. Pour the buttermilk into the well and mix with a fork to form a moist, sticky dough.

3. Drop 12 heaping tablespoons of the dough on an ungreased baking sheet, spacing the biscuits about 2 inches apart. Bake until the tops are tipped with golden brown, about 20 minutes. Serve warm. (Leftover biscuits, individually wrapped in aluminum foil, can be frozen for up to 1 month. Reheat the unwrapped biscuits in a preheated 400°F oven or toaster oven until thawed and hot, about 10 minutes.)

TROPICAL AMBROSIA

Fruit salad is a refreshing side dish. Ambrosia is **one of the best renditions,** but it doesn't have to include marshmallows and canned fruit. This one is packed with fresh fruits, along with cashews to add some crunch.

3 LARGE NAVEL ORANGES

3 RIPE MANGOES

1 RIPE PINEAPPLE, PEELED, CORED, AND CUT INTO BITE-SIZE PIECES

1 CUP SWEETENED FLAKED COCONUT (SEE NOTE)

GRATED ZEST AND JUICE OF 1 LIME

1 CUP COARSELY CHOPPED UNSALTED CASHEWS

1. To prepare the oranges, using a serrated knife, trim the top and bottom from an orange so it stands on the work surface. Cut off the peel with the pith where it meets the flesh. Working over a large bowl, cut between the membranes to release the orange segments. Discard the membranes. Repeat with the remaining oranges.

2. To prepare the mangoes, place a mango on the work surface. The pit runs horizontally through the center of the mango, with the flesh surrounding it. Using a sharp knife, cut off the top of the mango, just above the pit. Turn the mango over and repeat on the other side. Pare the mango flesh, cut into bite-size pieces, and add to the bowl with the oranges. The pit, with its clinging flesh can be pared and enjoyed as the cook's treat. Repeat with the other mango.

3. Add the pineapple, coconut, lime zest and juice to the oranges and mangoes, and mix gently. Cover and refrigerate until chilled, about 1 hour. (The ambrosia can be prepared up to 8 hours ahead, covered and refrigerated.) Just before serving, add the cashews and serve chilled.

Note: For an extraordinary ambrosia, substitute 1 cup freshly shredded coconut for the packaged coconut. To crack the coconut, working over a bowl to catch the juices, rap the coconut firmly around its equator with a hammer until it cracks. Pry out the coconut meat with a sturdy paring knife. Peel the coconut meat. Shred on the large holes of a food processor fitted with the grating disk. Freeze the leftover shredded coconut in an airtight container for up to 2 months.

FRESH-SQUEEZED LEMONADE

Handmade lemonade is **one of summer's greatest pleasures.** To reduce the elbow work, invest in an inexpensive electric ream juicer, or at least a Mexican lever-style juicer.

8 LARGE LEMONS

1 CUP SUGAR

FRESH MINT, FOR GARNISH

1. Squeeze the juice from the lemons, reserving the pulp and seeds. You should have 1¼ cups.

2. Transfer the juice, pulp, and seeds to a blender and add the sugar. Blend until the sugar is dissolved. Strain into a pitcher. Add 5 cups water and stir well. Serve over ice, garnished with the mint.

SUMMER BERRY SANGRÍA

Ripe summer berries add their juices to **this thirst-quenching favorite.**
To return the favor, the fruits are imbued with red wine, and make a delicious find at the
bottom of the glass. If you don't have superfine sugar, just process an equal amount of
granulated sugar in a blender or food processor until it is finely ground.

2 CUPS SLICED STRAWBERRIES

1 CUP FRESH RASPBERRIES

1 CUP FRESH BLUEBERRIES OR BLACKBERRIES

½ CUP SUPERFINE SUGAR

½ CUP RED RASPBERRY LIQUEUR OR ANY BERRY-FLAVORED SCHNAPPS

½ CUP BRANDY

ONE 1.5-LITER BOTTLE MERLOT, CHILLED

1. Gently mix the strawberries, raspberries, blueberries, sugar, liqueur, and brandy
together in a medium bowl. Cover and refrigerate until the berries are chilled and give off
their juices, at least 2 and up to 6 hours.

2. Mix the fruit and their juices with the wine in a large pitcher. Serve chilled, being sure
to include some fruit in each serving, with a single ice cube to avoid diluting the sangría.

INDEX